I0445321

Overcoming the Enemy's Plan

AN ANTHOLOGY

TENITA C. JOHNSON

Published by So It Is Written, LLC
Detroit, MI
SoItIsWritten.net

Overcoming the Enemy's Plan: An Anthology
Copyright © 2022 by Tenita C. Johnson

All rights reserved. No part of this book may be reproduced or transmitted in any form or by any means, electronic or mechanical, including photocopying, recording, or by an information storage and retrieval system—except by a reviewer who may quote brief passages in a review to be printed in a magazine or newspaper—without permission in writing from the publisher.

Edited by: So It Is Written – www.SoItIsWritten.net

Formatting: Ya Ya Ya Creative – www.YaYaYaCreative.com

ISBN: 979-8-9861260-3-6

LCCN: 2022914705

PRINTED AND BOUND IN THE UNITED STATES OF AMERICA

TABLE OF CONTENTS

FOREWORD

Prophetess Shawndra C. Johnson

 Have you ever felt like you were on the brink of something great? Something you know God created you to do?

However, there seems to be one problem: The devil has been hot on your tracks and just won't leave you alone! Instead of being excited about your calling, you are worried and doubtful. You even wonder if you heard God call your name at all!

Good news! (I heard you say, "Did she just say good news?") Yes! I said it, and I meant it. The good news is that your blessings and breakthroughs are at hand. You can feel it. But the devil knows it, too. He wants to do everything he can to thwart your destiny. What the enemy meant for evil God can, and will, turn it around for your good. He is going to make it work in your favor and give you double for your trouble.

You were never left alone. You weren't confused. There is nothing wrong with your hearing. You heard Him correctly.

It's just that the enemy heard Him, too. You are going to turn the world on its axis despite the opposition. Hold your head up high! Keep moving forward! Stand flat-footed and declare the Word of the Lord! Don't look back now because your mind-blowing destiny and blessings have arrived.

Congratulations! You have officially *Overcome the Enemy's Plan*!

Visionary Author Statement
UNDER THE COVERS

Tenita C. Johnson

 "If you have to do it in the dark … if you have to do it under the covers … if you have to do it when no one is home, it's sin."

That's what I heard the Lord say to me after I cleaned myself up for what I wanted to be the last time.

For years, I battled with whether or not watching porn and masturbating was a sin. After all, I knew married couples who agreed to watch porn together in order to "enhance" their marriage. That's what I convinced myself of in order to keep repeating the same cycle daily and, sometimes, hourly. Everyone was doing it. Saved

It wasn't fornication and it wasn't adultery because I wasn't married.

and unsaved friends and family alike told me it was okay. I even had a counselor tell me it was "normal" for women to pleasure themselves. That's when I knew it was time for me to find a new counselor.

When I was single, in my mind, I reasoned with God that watching porn and masturbating was much better than having sex with another man. It wasn't fornication and it wasn't adultery because I wasn't married. When I got married, I thought that would douse the flame of fire of lust that craved quenching daily every time I laid my head on the pillow or had an idle moment. However, my appetite increased all the more. Even after intimacy with my husband, two days later that appetite screamed louder than the moment before.

Unfortunately, over the years I'd programmed myself to be stimulated quickly, multiple times a day. That, in turn, left me always searching for the next high, the next hit, the next level of climax. I realized that I had committed adultery on my husband long before I had the extramarital affair after we'd been married ten years. In 1 Corinthians 7:4, the Word tells us, *The wife does not have authority over her own body but yields it to her husband. In the same way, the husband does not have authority over his own body but yields it to his wife.* According to this Scripture, I no longer had authority over my own body once I married. So, in essence, I may as well have been having sex with someone else's spouse!

As if that wasn't a big enough wakeup call for me, a pastor friend of mine told me that porn and masturbation was a form of prostitution. I was offended! I was appalled! *Was this joker calling me a prostitute?* I'd been many things in my lifetime. I'd even been called many things by many people.

One thing I never considered myself to be, though, was a prostitute. To make matters worse, he told me I was a prostitute working for free. After all, it didn't cost me money to touch myself and most porn I watched was on a DVD or free pay-per-view channels we had for the weekend.

Everyone is a slave to something or someone.

I thought that was enough to set me free, but I was only partially free. I didn't watch porn or masturbate daily. I graduated to the point where I may have only masturbated three times a week and watched porn twice a week. It truly depended on how busy I was (or was not). I learned early on in my adulthood why my fourth-grade teacher, Mrs. Cooper, used to say, "An idle mind is the devil's workshop." That was a big part of my problem. When I had hours of free time on my hands, masturbation or watching porn, and then taking a nap, was always the immediate suggestion from the inner me. So many people blame the enemy, Satan, for their problems. What I soon found out is that Satan only has to plant a seed, a thought, an idea, once for us to meditate on that thought before we act on it. Even with Satan's suggestions, we have a choice. We have free will. Everyone is a slave to something or someone. I realized that anything, or anyone, I listened to more than I did the voice of God became my god!

For me, that god was addiction to porn and masturbation—even in my marriage.

Eventually, I attended a benefit fundraiser for human trafficking, where victims shared their stories of living in hotel rooms and basements of homes for months. What I learned at that event was truly eye-opening. I didn't know that most of the women in porn are either underage or drugged and forced to perform for the camera. So, in essence, when I watched porn, not only was I committing adultery—but I was also silently supporting human trafficking. That was it for me. The women or girls in those films are someone's daughters. Those women and girls are someone's sisters. In order for me to be free, and absolutely free indeed, the Lord asked me some pretty bold questions.

If it separates you from God, it's sin.

"Would you masturbate in front of your husband or children?"

Hell no!

"Would you stand in the middle of someone else's bedroom and watch another couple have sex?"

God no!

"If you wouldn't do it in front of your husband or children, and if you wouldn't watch someone else have sex, then don't watch porn or masturbate. It's that simple."

See, if we listen for God's voice, we hear Him crystal clearly. We may not like what He says or how He says it. But we do hear Him. It's up to us to choose whether we will be slaves to sin or sold out for God and surrender all to Him!

If it separates you from God, it's sin. If He told you personally not to do something, and you do it anyway, it's disobedience, which is sin. If it brings you shame and embarrassment, it's sin. If you have to do it in the dark, it's sin. If you have to hide under the covers to do it, it's sin. I was in the church, singing in the choir and praise team, serving on youth ministry—operating in full sin. I was in the church building, but the church wasn't in me.

Today, I am not only an advocate who helps others heal from sexual abuse, but I also advocate for Christian women of all ages to break free and free indeed from the chains of pornography and masturbation addiction. Not everyone wants to be free. But I'm here for those who choose to live a life of freedom.

As you read the stories of these brave women who have not only overcome, but won, after having endured the enemy's plans for their life, lean in. Press in. Read it as if it was your story. Psalm 34:19 says, *Many are the afflictions of the righteous, but the LORD delivers him out of them all.*

Deliverance is available. Healing is available. Breakthrough is right at your doorstep. Afflictions may come, but rest in the fact that you have already won! Run your race with perseverance, knowing that the fight is fixed! You win in the end!

ABOUT THE VISIONARY AUTHOR

Tenita C. Johnson

Transforming pain into purpose is a gift that authorpreneur, speaker and book coach, Tenita "Bestseller" Johnson gives to everyone she encounters. She is a warrior of words with a fierce passion for guiding authors to expand their brand by showing them how to earn multiple streams of income from just ONE book. As the author of eighteen books, seven of which have been Amazon bestsellers, she is living proof that sharing your story leads to your destiny.

Familiar with rising from numerous fires and coming out unscathed, Tenita has triumphed over suicidal thoughts, depression, low self-esteem, marital storms and blended family woes. She has also endured miscarriages and the still birth of twins the day after she married her husband. Each of these tragedies has added indelible layers to her resilience. With more than 25 years in journalism, writing and editing, she has a knack for creating narratives that are authentic and raw, yet endearingly relatable. She is a vessel with the ability to change lives and impact the world, thus she is a proud "book bully," who relentlessly urges others to, "Write the book and get paid for the pain!"

When Tenita speaks, people listen with their ears as well as their hearts and souls because her transparency transcends pretense. She is a bold beacon of hope who inspires others to seek their highest peak. One of her proudest and defining moments was her appearance on Kirk Franklin's Praise Sirius XM channel.

As the founder and CEO of So It Is Written Publishing, she has helped hundreds of authors birth their books in record time. The 12-year-old company excels as a one stop shop for the complete book process from conception to completion, not just editing. The editorial guru successfully helps people to pen books that will boost their brand, accelerate their paydays and bust open doors of endless opportunities. So It Is Written won The Sunrise Pinnacle Award for Diversity Company of the Year, in 2020, from the Rochester Regional Chamber of Commerce in Rochester, Michigan. For six years, Tenita hosted the Red Ink Conference in Atlanta, Detroit, Charlotte and Chicago. Over 600 attendees received invaluable information from industry leaders on how to write, edit, market and publish their next bestseller.

Beyond her books, her versatility shines in multiple areas, including her role as the executive producer of the hit stage play, *When the Smoke Clears*, which was based on her book, *When the Smoke Clears: A Phoenix Rises*. The play ran in 2017 and 2018 to sold-out audiences in downtown Detroit. She also served as the editorial director for *Career Mastered Magazine* and *Hope for Women Magazine*. Currently, she is the national president of The Aspiring Writers Association of America, a writers' organization that collaborates with writers worldwide to pen their next literary masterpiece.

Tenita's passion for delivering bestselling books is matched only by her devotion to helping women and men heal from the drama, trauma and baggage of sexual abuse. Her 2021 anthology, *HUSH: Breaking the Cycle of Silence Around Sexual Abuse*, features eight women who lost their innocence and identity to life-altering trauma. She is a huge advocate and mouthpiece for those who have been sexually abused as she empowers them to release their pain instead of suffering in silence.

Her future plans include the release of *HUSH III*, producing her short film *What Happens in This House*, and completing the script for her feature film *When the Smoke Clears*. As a catalyst for positive change, she is a woman who has learned to live an intentional life of purpose while unapologetically fulfilling her God-driven assignments.

For booking or speaking engagements, email info@soitiswritten.net or visit www.tenitajohnson.com.

THE CHAIN BREAKER

Dr. Teresa Moore

"I ain't got no time to play bald-headed games with the devil!" From my very existence, that joka (the devil) has been trying to take me out. But God! Life for me hasn't always been pretty; in fact, it has been rough. The devil has always been trying to take something from me. First, it was my life. I was born a crack-addicted baby and all odds were against me. In the minds of physicians, and even some of my family members, survival was impossible for me. But God! What the enemy intended for evil, God turned for my good. God has turned my mourning into dancing.

I was born to two emotionally unavailable parents who set an insensitive, uninterested atmosphere for me, which caused me to be numb to emotions and hide behind a fake smile. My first encounter with feeling numb emotionally occurred when I was eight years old in a house on Francis Street in Pontiac, Michigan. Just thinking about that day still sends chills up and down my spine. The thoughts of the foul stench of his hot breath, his stubby calloused hands, and the drippings of Copenhagen tobacco in the corners of his mouth. Yuck! Why would an eight-year-old be eye candy for a grown man? It's beyond my thinking capacity. Yet, I found myself trapped underneath a perpetrator.

What was intended to be a day full of laughter turned out to be a nightmare that would be etched in my mind forever. It was a muggy, sweltering day in July. My curls had drawn up from the humidity and sweat dripped from my forehead. I sat anxiously waiting for my aunt's Volkswagen Beetle to pull up to my godmother's house so I could spend the day playing with my cousins. I was super excited for the visit. It had been months since I had seen them, and I was the only child living on the street. As soon as the car pulled up, I dashed off the porch and ran toward the curb to greet them. Oh, what a remarkable sight! We played kickball and hide-and-seek until the streetlights came on. Then, we all went inside the house to continue playing. Once inside the house, my godmother Flora instructed us to go upstairs to play. We had the time of our lives until my cousins became bored and called my aunt to come and pick them up.

Thirty minutes later, the Volkswagen pulled up again. All the children left the house, except me. I watched from the upstairs bedroom window as the yellow beetle zoomed down the street and out of my sight. I envisioned my aunt turning the car around and coming back to pick me up, but that never

"Don't say a word or I'm going to kill you," is what he whispered in my ear...

happened. I was left alone in an upstairs bedroom inside my godparents' home. They were passed out and intoxicated downstairs, along with several of their friends. I stood in the window for what felt like hours until it my eyelids became heavy. I turned the bedroom light off. The television illuminated the room as *Sanford and Son* played in the background.

Boom!

The bedroom door abruptly swung open and startled me. I gasped as I quickly turned toward the direction of the door. There stood an unidentified man who grabbed me and placed his hands tightly over my mouth while holding a knife.

"Don't say a word or I'm going to kill you," is what he whispered in my ear as I stood frozen, trying not to make a sound.

Oh, God! Help me! I screamed on the inside as he slid my pants down and threw me on the bed. I closed my eyes tightly. With his hot breath on my neck, and his grimy hands touching me, I felt sick! Next, he mashed my face and yelled, "Stay here! Don't move!" He released me and moved quickly out of the room toward the bathroom. My heart raced. I was scared, and I could feel urine running down my legs. *Where is my mommy and daddy? Where are my godparents? Who is going to help me?*

That's when it happened! I heard a noise outside and I jumped off the bed. I ran toward the window to see my dad's Cadillac pulling up. As he opened the car door, I yelled, "Daddy, help me!" He looked up in the direction of my screams and ran toward the house. He burst through the front door and bolted toward the stairs to the bedroom, just as the creepy rapist exited the bathroom.

Before my father said a word, the unidentified man yelled, "Tell them I didn't touch you! Tell them you are lying!"

The screams, the blood and the sounds of my dad's pointed-toe shoes stomping into the body of Mr. Creepy became a blur as my body became limp and I collapsed onto the floor. Somehow during the beating that my dad put on Mr. Creepy, my mother managed to call the police and EMS. When my eyes fluttered open, I was in the hospital and two police officers were waiting to ask me some questions. There was also a nurse and physician, ready to examine me. Mr. Creepy was going to jail and, for the next five days, I was in the hospital. The stress from the encounter sent me into shock. My body was full of infection and a boil the size of a golf ball developed on my outer left buttock.

The enemy tried to take my smile when the perpetrator placed his germ-infested hands over my mouth and took my innocence. The guilt and the shame that I felt was indescribable. I forced myself to smile on the outside as small pieces of me died daily. At a time when most children were running, happy and living their innocent lives, I was focused on not suffocating in my sorrows. Isaiah 43:2 says, *When you pass through the waters, I will be with you; and when you pass through the rivers, they will not sweep over you. When you walk through the fire, you will not be burned; the flames will not set you ablaze.* This is confirmation that God has been with me in every step of my journey. Also, it's confirmation that, even in the midst of my being violated, God is faithful. His love toward me is limitless. Even though I was a child, and I did not understand what happened to me, I am thankful that I survived the plans of the enemy. Today, my smile is no longer forced or fake. It is genuine. Every chance I get, I allow my lips to curve, my teeth to show, and my dimples to pop out. My smile looks good on me.

...God is faithful. His love toward me is limitless.

It was as if I had a target on my back. The enemy came hard after me consistently! Because I had such a stressful childhood, I promised myself that my children would not have to endure the hardships and disappointments I had to deal with. But what I did not know was that my seed would be a target of the enemy, as well.

I didn't grow up in church, but I was familiar with the devil and his job description. I also knew that he was not my friend. When Mr. Creepy violated me, according to physicians, there was a possibility that I would never carry a child. The devil is a liar! Since I was not bothering him, why was he bothering me and my seed? I discovered that I was pregnant with my daughter in February 1992 when I was rushed to the hospital. I was bleeding and having excruciating pain in my abdominal area. Little did I know, I was five months pregnant and in the process of miscarrying the baby. Well, *one of the babies.*

I found out hours later before a scheduled DNC that my daughter was hiding on my left side. I was pregnant with two babies and the sacs detached. Once again, God held back the hand of the enemy and saved my baby! Although I carried children in my womb who would eventually die at birth, God blessed my womb to carry my daughter. The Lord shut the mouths of the physicians who said I would not conceive and carry a child.

So, the enemy tried to take my life, my smile, my seed and, eventually, *my marriage!* Proverbs 18:22 (NLT) says, *The man who finds a wife finds a treasure, and he receives favor from the Lord.* God sent me my husband in November of 1994, right before Thanksgiving. Me and a friend of mine were at the *Nightriders* afterhours motorcycle club. A guy who I knew approached me to dance. After a few dances, he said he was coming home with me. I ignored his comments—until I walked out the club and he was in my car!

A year and a half later, we were married, and the enemy was on a mission to destroy what God joined together. To be honest, I played a role in helping the enemy. The "inner me" attacked my mind often. Romans 12:2 (NIV) says, *Do not conform to the pattern of this world but be transformed by the renewing of your mind.* I had much work to do. Due to my lack of not wanting to submit to authority, I lived a false reality. In my mind, I had a man, a family, and a thriving career. I was I-N-D-E-P-E-N-D-E-N-T! I was conformed to the world's view of things, which led me down a path of self-destruction. It wasn't until I grew tired of living a married life with a single mindset that I knew I had to shift. I was sick of self-sabotaging and causing unnecessary grief within myself. This time, it wasn't the enemy. It was the "inner me." I was so over being my own stumbling block. Just as a seamstress examines fabric and adjusts designs to create a professional, polished look, this is what God did for me when I surrendered to His will.

"I surrender!" is such a catchy phrase. I often wondered if Hillsong understood during the recording of their 2012 hit song the cost associated with the lyrics. I certainly did! Deciding to get serious about my relationship with God was the best choice I could have made. As God pulled back the layers, I saw an image of myself with which I was unfamiliar. He showed me, me! What I saw was not a pretty sight. I realized the enemy wasn't the only person working against me. I was working against myself. Surrendering is an important process of a renewed mindset. It requires a releasing of self, holding onto the Lord and allowing Him to be the light and the path.

Another step in the process of renewing one's mindset is to be willing to release the past. Don't allow trauma and disappointments to hold you hostage. This step was difficult for me. I didn't know how to release the pain I was exposed to when I was violated at eight years old. In my mind, I felt like everyone was out to hurt me as a child. That same mentality journeyed with me into adulthood. Trust wasn't something I ever mastered; I didn't trust others, nor did I trust myself. Proverbs 3:5 says, *Trust in the Lord with all your heart and lean not on your own understanding.* But how could I trust God? I couldn't see God! When I closed my eyes, I saw the creepy rapist. Where was God? Truth be told, God had been with me every step of the way. It was because He spared my life that I am here today. I am so thankful that God allowed me to survive that traumatic experience so I could witness the love of Jesus.

Knowing who we are in Christ, and what He has spoken concerning believers, is essential for a renewed mindset. As a child, I wasn't exposed to God's Word. However, as I grew older, I became curious. I learned early on that the *inner me*

> *Knowing who we are in Christ, and what He has spoken concerning believers, is essential for a renewed mindset.*

was stuck in places and spaces far too long. I was not using the tools allotted to me, including the Bible. Several times in Scripture, I read how the enemy tempted Jesus. On each occasion, Jesus responded with three words, *"It is written!"* Having knowledge of the written Word is what I used to wash my mind and to transform the way I viewed myself and others. I no longer hated the creepy man for violating me. I discovered that God loves me, and He calls me His own. For the first time in my life, someone was adding to me, not subtracting from me.

Although I was on a renewed mindset journey, I found myself easily offended--mostly because of the rejection and abandonment issues I suffered during childhood. I assumed everyone I came in contact with was a liar or manipulator. Mr. Creepy lied to the police officers when he told them he never touched me, and he wanted me to corroborate with his lies. The nerve! If I hadn't been pinned down under him before his bathroom break, I would have believed I was making the violation up. That is just how convincing his pleas were. This was the onset of the torture. I second guessed myself in every decision I needed to make. Mr. Creepy was the reason I felt the need to be validated, to prove that I was telling the truth, and that I was who I said I was. From time to time, I still suffer with the need to prove myself to others, even though God approves me. I swear by my word, and I pride myself on always fulfilling the things

I tell others I will do. I am known for showing up for others; however, when it is my turn for someone to show up for me, it rarely happens. I was so upset in the past until God reminded me that whatsoever service or deed I engage in, it was to be done as unto Him, not unto man. *Whoa!* That was a game-changing requirement. I had to do *everything* as unto the Lord. Jesus stood by His Word. John 6:63 tells us that the words He speaks unto us are spirit and life. Jesus reminds us that our words

I had to take a good look at myself and acknowledge what the enemy was doing. The enemy's job is to rob, steal, kill and to destroy.

carry life. We have the ability to speak life into the atmosphere and watch the harvest of those words manifest. Thus, I have adapted a lifestyle of commanding my day by speaking out God's promises and benefits that come along with having a relationship with Him. I no longer need to be validated by others. I am who God says I am, and I can do everything He said I could do.

Self-evaluation is key in mindset renewal. I had to take a good look at *myself* and acknowledge what the enemy was doing. The enemy's job is to rob, steal, kill and to destroy. He has done all of those things to me at one time or another. So, I had to be honest with myself and with God about what I really wanted in life. Mr. Creepy taught me by his actions how to devalue myself and my body. He stole my innocence as a child. As an adult, I didn't enjoy being intimate at all. In my mind, sex was disgusting and dirty. I imagined rough, stubby hands and foul breath anytime I was intimate, which immediately turned me off. I was introduced to sex at such a youthful age that I disassociated myself with all feelings and emotions related to it. To make matters worse, I was ashamed of my body image. Mr. Creepy planted that seed, and it was watered by several others who identified me as being *fat* with a pretty face. As if I had not gone through enough trauma, now I was dealing with self-esteem issues.

I spent several days miserable and crying because I hated the way my body was proportioned from a teen into adulthood. I tried everything to lose weight, every pill, intense exercises, and ridiculous diets. I had minimal results. Eventually, I reverted back to old habits. In September 2010, I had gastric lap band surgery and I lost forty pounds. Eventually, I gained twenty of the forty pounds back. In 2015, I had the lap band removed and the gastric sleeve procedure. Again, I lost seventy pounds, only to regain over half of the weight back. Surgery wasn't the answer; a renewed mindset was. I was so focused on altering my outer appearance, hoping the shame and self-blame would disappear with the weight, when the inner me was really what needed altering.

I am still struggling today with my weight; however, I have learned to love all of me and to work at losing one pound at a time. This time around, I am not looking for a quick fix. I realize I am worth doing the work for however long it takes.

God's Word has helped me remain confident in myself. I am victorious in Him, and I always win.

Finally, a renewed mindset requires having confidence in yourself. After the violation, I struggled with confidence in God and myself for years. It wasn't until my relationship with God grew that I understood He knows everything about me. There is nowhere that I can go, and He is not there. Psalm 139 reminds us that God searches us and that He is aware of our every movement; thus, we can be assured that He will come through for us. I used to look at God through the same lenses I looked at man with. God supersedes every thought and imagination I have concerning Him. I have taken on the Apostle Paul's positioning in Romans 8:38: *For I am convinced that neither death nor life, neither angels nor demons, neither the present nor the future, nor any powers, neither height nor depth, nor anything else in all creation, will be able to separate us from the love of God that is in Christ Jesus our Lord.* God's Word has helped me remain confident in myself. I am victorious in Him, and I always win. I may face challenges and afflictions, but I have been promised to come through unscathed.

Reflection Questions

1. *How does a renewed mindset directly affect how we view the challenges we encounter?*

_____

_____

_____

2. *What are the necessary steps in the renewed mindset process?*

_____

_____

_____

3. *Why is a transformed mindset necessary to heal?*

_____

_____

_____

ABOUT THE AUTHOR

Dr. Teresa Moore

*A*ffectionately known by many as The Purpose Pusher, Dr. Teresa Moore knows firsthand what it's like to deal with rejection, hurt and abuse. More importantly, she knows what it feels like to overcome that much and more. Strategic about helping others identify and change toxic behavior, her desire to see people happy, healed, and whole shines brightly for all to see—in and outside the four walls of the church.

As a community agent of change, minister and mental health professional, Dr. Moore takes pride in sowing seeds of hope and love throughout Pontiac, Michigan, and surrounding areas. As the owner and operator of Emages Counseling and Advocacy Services, she offers a variety of therapeutic services, including but not limited to individual, married and group counseling; assessments; and educational treatment services to clients and families in the time of crisis. She has over 29 years of extensive experience working with the developmentally disabled and mentally challenged population in various leadership roles.

Holding both a Ph.D. in Religious Education, and a Master of Counseling, she prides herself on masterfully combining the Word of God with psychological processes and procedures to help her clients break free from past wounds and hurts that continue to hold them hostage. In her work as an adjunct professor, Dr. Moore uses a connective instructional style called "Living Life with your Hands Wide Open." Serving in multiple capacities of help and customer service, she seeks to go above and beyond the normal call of duty—and encourages her students and mentors to do the same.

Dr. Moore pinned her first book *Awakened to Win* in April of 2020. This book is filled with daily affirmations and prayers that are sure to jumpstart your day. She was also a co-author in several anthologies, including *Gathering the Fragments, Living and Loving Life Without Regrets,* and *Recrowning God's Daughters.* Affiliated with numerous professional and community organizations, such as the American Counseling Association, *Psychology Today,* NOHS, HUS Club, the American Red Cross and Delta Sigma Theta Sorority, Inc., Dr. Moore is sure to bring life to any dead situation she encounters.

Having received the Professional Women's Club Shero Award twice, her creative ability to deliver resources, encouragement and strength to men and women who are at the end of their rope leads them to find their God-given purpose and passion. Serving under multiple ministries at The River, New Wine Glory Ministries, on the board of The Fountain for Women, Ruth and Naomi Ministries or Kingdom Carriers, it is crystal clear that she not only loves God—but she also loves His people and wants what is best for every one of them.

Whether she's co-hosting "Be in the Drivers Seat" radio show on Detroit Praise Network 99.9, hosting her signature "Write the Vision! Work the Plan!" vision board workshop or participating in the annual "7-Up Service," attendees are sure to leave empowered and inspired to know that they are born with greatness within—they simply need to tap into it!

For more information or interviews, email dr.teresamoore@gmail.com or visit her www.drteresamoore.com. Connect with her on Facebook @DrTeresa Moore or on Instagram @dr.teresa_moore.

THE MAKING OF A QUEEN

Regina Eileen Woodard

Tuesday, April 16, 2006, was a breezy morning. I could hear birds chirping in the background as I stood over the kitchen sink washing dishes. I woke up feeling good that morning and smiled softly as I inhaled the spring-scented Dawn dish soap. My oasis was short-lived when the phone rang and jolted me back to reality. Hot water splashed on my face as I reached for the telephone. It was my aunt Annette Dempsey. We exchanged pleasantries.

Then, time stood still as my core shook. I could hear my aunt talking; however, I didn't understand the words coming through the telephone. *Was I hearing her correctly? Nah, I had to be dreaming!* My heart leapt out of my chest as I opened my mouth and screamed.

"Not my Daddy!"

She couldn't be talking about my hero, my protector, my best friend. This was the day my whole world changed. Since then, I have not been the same.

✻ ✻ ✻ ✻ ✻

I was born in the city that was birthed in 1818, named after a war chief of the Ottawa Tribe called Pontiac. Pontiac was known in the 20th Century for its General Motors manufacturing plants. At 6:55 a.m., on a warm, muggy July 25,1969, the queen was born at St. Joseph Mercy Hospital. I was born nine pounds and fifteen inches to proud parents, Mr. and Mrs. Chesley Woodard, Sr.

My parents decided they couldn't let go of the dream of having a precious little girl,…

Things were not always 'peaches and cream' in the Woodard household. Born before me were my two brothers, Chesley, Jr., who was the oldest, and Bruce Eric. In the 60s, doctors didn't have the technology to diagnose and inform a parent early on that their child was going to have special needs. Back then, people with special needs were referred to as 'retarded,' which made an already difficult situation even more challenging with this negative stigma.

For years, my parents wrestled with the dream of having a little girl. Given the circumstances, they were unsure if having a third child was the right thing to do. Prior to my birth, my parents were devastated because of a miscarriage after twelve weeks of pregnancy. My mother sought to numb the pain of losing the third child by taking her body into another pregnancy. My parents decided they couldn't let go of the dream of having a precious little girl, even if it meant trying four more times and not being successful.

When I was eleven years old, I was teased and bullied by one of my schoolmates for two years. I hated school. Every day, I dreaded walking through the doors of that school building because I knew I would be the bully's target. To make matters worse, I was one of the tallest kids in the school. Thus, my tormentor gave me the nickname "Lurch." Daily, I wanted to smash his face with my fist so he could experience the same embarrassment as I did. Not only did the bullying affect me in school, but also at home. I had nightmares several times a week and I wet the bed regularly, compounding the trauma. I could hear the word "Lurch" repeatedly in my head as I cried myself to sleep many nights.

Every day that I rode the school bus, my bully called me Lurch. Lurch was a fictional character created by American cartoonist, Charles Adams, as a manservant to The Addams Family. During this time in my life, my mom and dad did what all parents would do. They went to the school and met with the teachers and principals, but there was no resolution and the bullying continued. I knew I was different. I was 5'11", and I wore a size twelve shoe at eleven years old, the same height and shoe size I am today.

To help deal with my self-esteem issues, our family went to church every Sunday together. My dad decided that I needed to get more involved with my peers at church and he wanted me to join the choir. I could not hold a note, let alone remember the words to songs. But my dad took me to choir rehearsal and stayed with me every Wednesday for one year until I was okay with being left alone with my peers at church. Even singing in choir became a nightmare in my mind because I always imagined someone in the choir teasing me and making fun of my big feet and height.

Soon after, my father also introduced me to basketball as a tool to help me release pain and gain confidence. The love of the game is what helped me find my way and shape me into the woman I am today. Although my father did his best to get me to leave all my anger on the court, my pent-up anger was unleashed when, one day, my foot met the face of my childhood enemy. It was a great day.

Challenges continued in my life during my senior year of high school. It was time to prepare for the next chapter of my life. During this time, everyone was preparing to work or take up a trade. Some became entrepreneurs and some were preparing to take the ACT. I took the ACT, but I did not meet the requirements to attend a four-year school. My scores were so low that *...I woke up one burning Monday morning and decided that I no longer wanted to live and work in the shadow of the 'Old Boys Club'.* I ended up at a junior college and played basketball for two years. I finished my schooling at a four-year college. Despite my college basketball scholarships, I fell under Proposition 48, a controversial regulation that mandated minimum high school student grades and scores on the standardized college entrance exams for the student-athletes to participate in sports. This rule went into effect in 1986, a year before I graduated from high school. This was another major disappointment. I was in the low tier of my classes as an average C-student.

The enemy wanted me to throw in the towel. I cried too many tears and worked too hard to quit. On June 15, 1998, I started working in an industry that is known to many as the 'Old Boys Club'. This 'club' is still in existence today, but it is getting better. This 'club' was a group of wealthy men with similar beliefs and educational backgrounds. If you didn't look, walk or talk like them, you did not fit in.

In 2012, I woke up one burning Monday morning and decided that I no longer wanted to live and work in the shadow of the 'Old Boys Club'. I wanted to work for an owner who owned fifteen dealerships and eighteen brands, not realizing however that racism was looming around the corner and waiting to strike me to the ground. But I had to turn to what my dad taught me as a little girl: to always look to my faith and never run from the devil. He taught me to face his tail head on and, at the same time, give it all to the Lord.

In June of 2012, my second day on the job, I noticed everyone was driving a 'demonstrator' or 'demo car', which is what we call today a 'company car.' I was the finance manager, and all my peers and salespeople rolled into work in their new cars if they worked in new car sales. If they worked in the pre-owned department, they drove a slightly used car. In order for me to drive a company car, we had to sell thirty cars consistently for sixty days. In my interview, management told me that no one drove a company car. They had allegedly stopped letting employees drive company cars six months prior.

The used car department that I worked in consisted of three finance managers and no salespeople. Our job was to generate sales by marketing to customers with our own advertising budget. In our first month, we sold thirty-two cars. In the second month, we sold thirty-nine cars, with no company car for me in sight.

During my tenure at this dealership, I met a lady named Crystal Williams, who I became acquainted with through Pontiac Meals on Wheels nonprofit. We both sat on the fundraising committees. Crystal, who is the President & CEO of Crystal Vision Communications, LLC, has a background in public relations, but her specialty is taking a client's vision, transforming it into reality, and delivering exceptional results. Crystal took my niche of helping individuals with bruised credit get into cars and helped make me a household name. This was when "The Queen of Car Loans" brand was birthed.

It's about character and responsibility.

Crystal bought into the vision that The Queen of Car Loans was the person who would listen to your problems, then figure out a plan to turn your bus pass into keys to your new or used car. If you couldn't get into a car right away, then we worked on a plan to help you get your credit in order to purchase that new or used car. While developing my niche, and working with people who had bruised credit, those who went through divorce, those who lost their job, and those whose income changed, I started a nonprofit called Queens Future Successors. Our organization strives to serve generations of youth and families to strengthen our communities by offering an array of educational financial literacy workshops.

I started my nonprofit because, over the years, I encountered many customers who did not plan or properly prepare for their future financially. I figured that if I started with the younger generation, they could teach their parents. I also realized that teaching kids how to handle money is about more than dollars and cents. It's about character and responsibility. According to Raj Chetty, Stanford economist, "Approximately 60 percent of children from the poorest families are working at age 30, compared with 80 percent of children from median income families."

Today, I can be seen in TV, print, social media and radio advertisements. I currently host my own weekly radio show, *Be in the Drivers Seat*, which comes on every Saturday morning at 8:30 a.m. on the Detroit Praise Station. For two years, I've also had my own infomercial where I walked people through the process of buying a new or used car. To this day, I am blessed to have a huge customer base that comes through advertising, word of mouth, and people simply walking in and saying, "I am here for the queen!" My tenure at the large dealership was not in vain. I became a household name. Today, when a person thinks of cars, they think of Regina, the Queen of Car Loans.

On January 2, 2008, at 5:13 a.m., raindrops hit the hospital window. I also heard the nurse's alarm on her watch go off as she woke me up to tell me that my dad had passed. This was the day I put my head on my father's lap for the last time. It was when I prayed for the last time *for him* instead of *with him*. I asked for one hour to let him know that I finally understood why God called him home. My dad's time on this side of the earth was completed and, in my opinion, he got an A+ for the assignment. My dad raised his three children, and I believe he was finally at peace with knowing that his baby girl was no longer a princess, but she had developed into a queen.

Reflection Questions

1. *Have you ever been bullied? If so, what's one way your bully has made you stronger?*

_____

_____

_____

_____

2. *When you were at your lowest point in life, what's one person who was there for you and how?*

_____

_____

_____

_____

3. *Did/do you have an outlet in your life? If so, what is it and how does it help you?*

_____

_____

_____

_____

4. *My number one strength is connecting with people and building relationships. What's yours and are you focusing on your number one skill in life? If not, what's one way you can start focusing and spending time today on your number one strength?*

_____

_____

_____

_____

5. *What's the one dream you've always had that you've yet to act on? What's one action or step you can take today to move you toward your dream?*

_____

_____

_____

_____

ABOUT THE AUTHOR

Regina Eileen Woodard

*P*erseverance past shaky circumstances is why Regina Woodard is known as The Queen of Car Loans, with well over two decades of experience within automotive sales and finance. Yet, her mission entails more than securing deals, as she has a relentless passion for helping others achieve financial literacy. As an African American woman in male-dominated industries, she offers remarkable impact and influence.

Familiar with overcoming adversity, her tenacious spirit was built during her formative years when her peers bullied her. Her brand represents integrity and a fierce commitment to giving her best, deeming her a top earner at Joe Lunghamer Chevrolet in Waterford, Michigan. She has generated a steady stream of clientele, and through her expertise in all things credit, 60 to 70% of her customers successfully purchase vehicles. She regularly appears in TV commercials for the dealership and can also be heard on radio ads via Beasley Media Group.

Regina shares her expertise on cars and credit through her YouTube channel, Regina the Queen of Car Loans and Credit and also weekly on Be in the Drivers Seat, on Detroit's The Praise Network.

The Pontiac, Michigan native's nonprofit 501(c)(3), Queens Future Successors, focuses on teaching youth in the community the importance of having good financial health by starting the process at a young age. She is driven to pave the way for future generations by ensuring they are prepared to compete with their counterparts. Her collaborations include the Pontiac School District.

Regina remains connected to her community via her affiliations with the Pontiac Meals on Wheels program and as a member of the Regional Chamber of Commerce. Known for her honesty and candor, she shares her ascension above obstacles meant to stop her in "Overcoming the Enemy's Plans," an anthology available in the fall of 2022.

OVERCOMING THE ENEMY'S PLAN

Shonda D. Gibbs

 I was a single twenty-four-year-old living with my three-year old son, Quentin, when I experienced my first demonic encounter. A supernatural confrontation that I never told anyone about, not even the pastor, believing he would not believe me. Although I grew up and served in the church, never have I heard about this type of manifestation occurring in the lives of believers or even know how to respond to it.

On the night previously mentioned, I was sitting up in bed reading. The lamp on the nightstand was lit, and the townhome was quiet. Quentin was asleep in his room. For some reason, I felt uneasy trying to focus on my reading as I experienced an increase in anxiety. Soon, I found myself fighting the heaviness of allowing myself to drift off to sleep. Moments passed as the ability to stay awake became harder. Still in the same position, my eyelids were heavy. Within seconds of closing my eyes and opening them again, this is what I saw and heard:

An image of a dark red and black face with piercing eyes was floating right before me. In sheer terror the ability to scream was prohibited. The entity spoke, "You cannot have her. She belongs to me." The sound of its words slithered from its mouth. Baffled at what was stated, I instantly recalled a conversation with a family member regarding salvation and baptism. The spirit leaned in closer inches from my face and snickered mocking me because I was talking to others about Jesus. The manifested presence of the enemy speaking to me face-to-face was incomprehensible as it lingered long enough to complete its mission – to instill fear. Hearing its words were cunning, manipulative, and deceptive. Fear attached itself deep inside me settling itself as a stronghold.

...my journey in recognizing the need for deliverance and the ability to overcome his satanic schemes against me and my destiny in Christ.

As quickly as the spirit came, it was gone.

This disturbing and impactful moment never left me. The supernatural encounter has reminded me over the years, as I have grown and matured in understanding the dynamics of the Kingdom of Heaven and the development of my personal relationship with the Lord Jesus Christ through the Holy Spirit, the spirit realm is real. Fifteen years later, the spirit of fear and the satanic forces of darkness working with this stronghold, or strongman, returned with a vengeance against my life!

Vivid details concerning these spiritual encounters are explained in my first debut book, *"What Does Thou Seeth – The Emergence of a Seer."* Depending on the context and according to Webster's and Oxford dictionaries a stronghold is defined as a place:

- That has been fortified so as to protect it against attack

- Where a particular cause or belief is strongly defended or upheld

- Of security or survival

Here is a dream entry from *"What Does Thou Seeth,"* providing a detailed visual by the Holy Spirit in revealing my stronghold and what it looked like symbolically. This is the beginning of my journey in recognizing the need for deliverance and the ability to overcome his satanic schemes against me and my destiny in Christ.

The Basement

"Walking through my current and dimly lit home, I heard muffled sounds coming from the kitchen that distracted me. Since I was the only one in the house, I was concerned about what I heard. I went to investigate. As I entered the kitchen, a small glimpse of light peered from the slightly closed curtains over the kitchen sink. It was the only illumination that was provided to help me navigate through the area. Before I could say "Hello," an eeriness overcame me. Something was not right. Fear gripped me as I slowly and hesitantly walked toward the basement stairs. I heard the muffled sounds again. Someone is in my basement!? Scared, confused, and bewildered to what to do, I made my way to the landing of the stairwell.

There two dark images stood tall and strong, boldly preventing me to proceed. Intimidation and fear literally brought me to my knees before I clearly heard the faint and weak voice crying out, "Help me." It was a plea for help. Attempting to get away from the terrifying entities, I went through the house towards the front door, surprisingly realizing it was cracked open. Seeing the light penetrating from the crevasse, a brief sense of freedom entered my heart until the front closet slowly opened. A darker, much more evil presence emerged, stopping me quickly in my tracks. Without fully exposing itself, revealing only its eyes, it spoke directly to me, tormenting with the words, "I will not let you go." I woke up.

I can share a significant amount of life altering moments in life including *after* receiving salvation. Molestation, being raped repeatedly for an entire night bound to a bed, years of psychological and emotional abuse in marriage, homelessness, infidelity and much more resulted in a slow dismantling of who I was as a person and as a woman. More importantly, it dismantled who I was created to be in Christ Jesus. While many believers in Christ look at the fruit or the symptoms (things happen in life or brought on by the enemy of Christ) somehow, I have a spiritual gift to discern the *source* operating behind the life of an individual dictating and influencing their thoughts, beliefs, and behaviors.

As believers, how can you overcome an unseen enemy who systematically plots against you?

"Satan, who is the god of this world, has blinded the minds of those who don't believe. They are unable to see the glorious light of the Good News. They don't understand this message about the glory of Christ, who is the exact likeness of God."
–2 CORINTHIANS 4:4 (NLT)

How am I able to discern? It is through the divine enablement of Christ. As believers, how can you overcome an unseen enemy who systematically plots against you? Are you aware there are over six thousand demonic spirits that are assigned to hold a person hostage preventing the individual from walking in the full statue of Christ? Although, spiritual giftings have been dispersed individually as the Spirit of the Lord willed (1 Corinthians 12), the admonishment to walk in the vocation in which we have been called (Ephesians 4:1), and an order established in perfecting of the saints, work of the ministry to edify the Body of Christ (Ephesians 4:11-13) there is a hidden satanic diabolical plot against the people of God and the agenda of the Kingdom of Heaven!

Scripture cautions us to, *"Be sober (well balanced and self-disciplined), be alert and cautious at all times. That enemy of yours, the devil, prowls around like a roaring lion (fiercely hungry), seeking someone to devour"* (1 Peter 5:8, AMP). There should come a point in our Christian walk when the responsibility in examining ourselves for spiritual growth and maturity is vital for the glory of the Lord to be revealed in and through our lives. This is done by allowing the work of Holy Spirit to shine the light in any, and all, areas of darkness we may have given place for the enemy to dwell. Our unseen enemy seeks to "devour." The Greek word of devour is *katapiein*, literally meaning to "swallow" or to "drown." The agenda of the enemy is designed to damage our faith, preventing us from walking in obedience in Christ. He lies to distort our understanding of the character and nature of Christ. He has an insatiable desire to rob us of experiencing the bountiful blessings made available, walking in power and authority, and continuing the work of Jesus which is to spread the Gospel!

> *The agenda of the enemy is designed to damage our faith, preventing us from walking in obedience in Christ.*

The enemy is referred to as a "thief" in Scripture. He comes subtly to steal joy, hope, faith, identity, destiny, and purpose while God sent Jesus to give us life more abundantly in every area. For decades, while serving and attending church services, praying for others, and identifying as Christian, my ignorance to the movement of darkness against my life increased. These experiences were terrifying, as well as paralyzing, resulting in the hindrance of not only my spiritual growth and maturity, but my belief in the Word of the Lord spoken over my life.

The Manifestations of the Spirit of Fear

It has taken me ten years to recognize and receive the revelation from the Lord that the strongman of fear has been holding me hostage preventing me from living a life of freedom in Christ in the mind, soul, and spirit. Can you imagine my response when I realize the silent cries from "The Basement" dream was me? Evidently, I must be an asset in ministry and to the Kingdom of Heaven. An entire chapter in *"What Does Thou Seeth"* gives an extensive and insightful view of the demonic encounters of the mental torment that has kept me hostage.

The manifestations of the strongman are the following:

- Mental silent torment

- Untrusting/doubt

- Excessive timidity

- Fear of man

- Anxiety/stress

The enemy is subtle in all of his ways. He is "clever, elusive, cunning, devious, crafty." Matthew 24:24 mentions the dept of deception regarding even the very elect (of Christ) can be tricked, hoodwinked, or bamboozled to the schemes of the enemy. These tactics listed in the bullets had a significant impact on my mental, emotional, psychological, and physical areas of my life.

It all started when my husband's health was in trouble early in our marriage. Sporadic visions were revealed at this time, even though I had no clue what many of them were conveying. Due to this ignorance, I took one vision literally, and it kept me bound, living in daily torment as to what was to come.

In August of 2008, a vision was revealed where my husband was violently killed. The vivid details of the image left me with a spirit of torment. Day by day, for over a year, the spirit visited my heart and mind, reminding me of the dream, inviting the spirit of anxiety to bring an aggravated mental disturbance. Can you imagine worrying if your husband will make it home from work? Think about waiting for a police officer to come to your door to tell you your husband was in an automobile accident. I was held captive in the mind, with limited power to activate the Word of God, not only in my life, but the life of my husband. I was terrified! We both attended church services, serving in various ministry assignments. Yet, the enemy was holding both of us hostage. There is more to this story to enlighten our understanding to the doors we all leave open for the enemy to come in, reside, and/or wreak havoc in every area of our lives.

The attacks were so consistent to ensure there was no authentic development of joy, faith, worship, commitment, the Word of God, and freedom in Christ. Allow me to expound a little bit more in another vision shared in *"What Does Thou Seeth"* about how the enemy attempted, and honestly succeeded, to arrogantly telling me, and my spouse that we had no power against him.

The Little Girl on the Porch

"My husband and I were sitting in our dimly lit living room. I was laying on my back on the floor, while Herman was relaxing on a sectional sofa in front of the window when we heard a noise from outside. We both jumped up as I ran to the door. He jumped over the couch to arrive at the front door as soon as I did. When I opened the door, there was a young Caucasian girl, standing in a white dirty dress, crying. Quickly exiting the house to approach the child, my attention was diverted to an image of a person walking along the sidewalk who later stopped midway from

It spoke directly to me. "You do not have power over me because I am still in you."

our driveway and kneeled. Simultaneously, an old pick-up truck slowly down our street when it came to a halt aligning with the individual kneeling. From the opposite direction, another image of person arrived and kneeled. These three figures stood on the perimeter of our property.

Returning my attention to the young girl, she started to convulse and dropped to the porch on her back. Her small body shook, and her eyes rolled into the back of her head. Quickly at her side to *Overcoming the plan of the enemy is not easy.* provide aid, the moment changed. The young girl swiftly stood up, focused and alert, as if nothing happened. Herman stood in the doorway as I welcomed the child into our home. As soon as she crossed the threshold, the girl hastily retreated to the porch. The child turned toward me and transformed into a face of a demon. It spoke directly to me. "You do not have power over me because I am still in you." He turned to Herman and said, "The same with you." The enemy looked over my right shoulder, nodded his head (as to point something out) and with all the hatred it could express continued, "I can't touch him because the Word covers him." Even though Joshua our youngest child was not present, within this vision, I discerned the demon was referencing him. The entity rolled his eyes in disgust as the spirit returned its gaze on me to reiterate, we did not have power!

The stronghold of the spirit of fear impacted my life and spiritual development to the point it left me with another internal struggle: recognizing I did not have power as I examined my choices, behaviors, and seeing the fruit in my marriage, finances, children, and mental wellbeing. I was embarrassed, tormented, and broken pondering the encounter and message the enemy presented. The enemy was bold enough to visit, disguising himself as someone innocent, before revealing his true nature. Although the message was concerning me, my spiritual maturity and lack of authority in Christ, through the revealing of Holy Spirit, there are many who profess Christ, but only live a form of godliness with *no authentic* power in Christ Jesus. (2 Timothy. 3:5).

This message was not just for me, but for many to truly examine themselves in Christ to assess behaviors, thought processes, and lifestyle to ensure it matches the nature and characteristics of Christ and what God requires to be identified as one of His. People honor Him with their lips, but He says, *"Their hearts are far from me"* (Matthew 15:8).

Overcoming the plan of the enemy is not easy. We see the acts of Satan illustrated throughout scripture from Elijah outrunning Jezebel, Jesus and the Apostles enduring extensive persecution, the enemy tormenting Paul, the Apostle, to the Lord granting permission for the enemy to test Job. We must be careful in our estimation in determining what manifestations are from the enemy, in which we have granted him access, to the Lord giving him permission to bring testing in the life of a person. To overcome the plans of the enemy one must be intentional in worship unto the Lord in humility, honor, and integrity. God seeks true worshippers (John 4:23). One has to be intentional to walk and live in implicit and explicit obedience in Christ Jesus to ensure all doors are closed for the enemy to enter. These individuals are actively engaged in daily living to honor the Lord in everything they do from studying, meditating, and *living* the Word of God, singing praises to Him, and rejoicing in knowing intimately the One in which they serve.

After extensive demonic encounters over the years and the silent torment, I was finally in a place in Christ to be able to receive and interpret this next vision God lovingly revealed for me to gain ground and victory over the enemy.

"Study the Enemy"

"I was in my bedroom laying across the bed, relaxed. The room was dark, and the door was open. I sensed someone else was in the room with me. I was engaged with the person in laughter before an item fell on the floor, distracting me. As I reached down to grab the object, the person quickly came from behind and softly whispered in my ear, "Shhh! Listen." The person directed my attention toward the doorway. Standing up, I cautiously walked toward the bedroom door into the hallway. The house was dimly lit, allowing me the ability to see. Entering in the living area, there I stood, astonished at what I saw! In the top

Standing still, afraid to move, I followed the instructions given.

corner of my dining room, a huge "crablike" creature with long spiked legs and beady eyes looking around, anticipating his next move without being caught. Stunned by the appearance and its presence, the person with me leaned in and whispered in my ear again, "Don't move."

Standing still, afraid to move, I followed the instructions given. I watched the creature slowly and gradually climb down the wall, positioning himself boldly on the floor. He quickly looked around again to ensure it was safe to proceed.

Instantly, the scene changed.

"I was transmigrated back into my bedroom – waiting on the next move from the enemy. I heard his subtle movements as he made his way down the hallway toward my direction. The peaceful presence reminded me to remain quiet and focus while I kneeled to pray. "Pay attention." The creature approached and entered the bedroom doorway. Surprisingly, the creature appeared as though he could not see me; was it looking for someone? Why would he be here in the room? The enemy was

now face to face with me, mere inches from touching one another. The friendly presence remained close with me, leaned in and whispered in my ear from behind.

"Don't move; study his movements."

I awoke.

The spirit of fear does not come from the Spirit of God, but "love, power, and a sound mind" (2 Timothy 1:7) does.

There is freedom in Christ Jesus!

Recognizing the source and the time of entry of this spirit to the power of Christ becoming more pronounced in my life gave me the divine enablement to gain victory! I thank God for the grace, the activation of His Word, and the dismantling process against the strongman assigned to my life. I repented to the Lord for the doors open knowingly and unknowingly, where I allowed the enemy to come in.

In maintaining deliverance, work is still required. Luke 11:26, NIV states, *"Then it goes and takes seven other spirits more wicked than itself, and they go in and live there. And the final condition of that person is worse than the first."*

It is imperative not to see or respond to the spirit of fear arbitrarily but to recognize the source in which it manifest and the course it is intended to make. There is freedom in Christ Jesus!

 *Reflection Questions*

1. *What areas are still exposed in your life for the enemy to have access to?*

    _____

    _____

    _____

2. *What doors do you need to repent for leaving open for the enemy to gain entry?*

    _____

    _____

    _____

3. *How does your lifestyle, mannerisms and actions reflect the nature of Christ?*

    _____

    _____

    _____

ABOUT THE AUTHOR

Shonda D. Gibbs

$\mathcal{W}$hile many people seek platforms, titles and greater accolades, Shonda Gibbs realizes that her purpose is in serving others, not being served. As co-founder and program director of "We Care Connect Memory Café," a community program that is provided to caregivers and persons living with memory loss to engage in social conversation and entertaining activities while developing friendships for mutual support. For over ten years, Shonda has faithfully volunteered with non-profit organization Paula Ratchford Ministries in various local outreach programs and foreign mission endeavors to aid the most vulnerable populations including individuals and families experiencing homelessness, "at-risk" youth and young adults, and victims of human trafficking.

With a heart for evangelism, Shonda has faithfully served in various leadership roles and outreach programs as near as her hometown of Ypsilanti, Michigan to as far as Madrid, Spain. Shonda is on a mission to transform lives through her transparency. She is an emerging seer of the Lord Jesus

Christ who desires for many to recognize the purposeful work of the Holy Spirit within their hearts, while helping them to discern His voice and become captivated by His drawing power to live in life union with Him.

Our Story in Black and White

BEING A BILLBOARD
FOR CHRIST

Pastor Lisa Reeves

 Picture this: When two different worlds suddenly come together (collide) to produce such strength, confidence and love—all to build a great example. Not knowing, nor realizing, through the different backgrounds, the different cultures, the different foods, the different up-bringing, the different religious beliefs, all the way to different hair textures that the Lord would use all of these differences for His glory. I'm honored to see that the Lord would, did and has continued to use us as *His billboard*!

I've heard from painters (artists) and photographers that in order to develop a photo in black and white, one must remove any distraction of color. This helps the viewer focus on other aspects of the picture. For example, the pattern, the subject, the major advantage that black and white together brings to the forefront. There is a beautiful light and rich texture that yields a strong, but wonderful mood, when one looks at it.

I'm not talking about the paintings at the art museum or photos taken years ago (which are usually classics) that people travel for miles to an auction to see. I'm not talking about the paintings that people negotiate large crazy amounts of money for. I'm talking about when Rob and I met, became friends, and fell hard for each other.

I was just hanging with some friends at the mall when this *cute* guy walked up. He was looking for one of our friends. All I could see was his blue eyes. "Hello," is what he said when he walked directly up to me. Looking up at him, because he was tall and built like a statue, I said, "Hey! What's up?" I had the biggest smile on my face, and I bat my eyelashes.

This was the beginning of an amazing, unusual, fun and different relationship. Here was this guy whom I'd met. Right away, I noticed and was attracted to his laugh, his not-so-funny jokes, his kind heart and his manners. He was a complete gentleman.

As the daughter to two old-school southern parents, that's what I was used to: charm and people being polite. It's hard to explain how incredible our conversations were. We sat on the phone for hours, even while we watched TV. Of course, we were watching the same show.

From the beginning, we had straight, honest, sometimes difficult talks. We found a way to answer the not-so-easy questions. When Rob and I starting dating, we agreed to always ask instead of assuming.

We were from two different worlds. Spending so much time with each other gave us such an opportunity to learn each other; it felt so natural. It wasn't about laughing or judging something we weren't familiar with, but we were careful not to hurt each other's feelings. As the Bible says, "In all thy getting, get an understanding." We are an interracial couple. Robert is a Caucasian man, who was raised as a Jehovah's Witness. He is really quiet and shy. He tried his hardest to dress to impress, and he went to school in the suburbs. He only knew Jesus as a teacher. Then, there's me: a Black woman who is loud and funny, who dresses to impress every time and everywhere I go. I am an in-your-face, taking-no-mess-from-nobody PK (preacher's kid). I was raised in the church, I love Jesus, and I know Him as my Lord and Savior.

We were from two different worlds.

But our differences made us so amazingly peculiar. Just like the definition for peculiar, when people saw us, they saw unexpected, strange, puzzling, baffling, extraordinary, funny things happen. All Rob and I saw was each other's hearts. As we introduced ourselves to the other family,

including our parents, this is where
the color (the distractions) started.

*...Rob had questions
about Jesus. He
enjoyed the joy and
love that he felt
when he was with me
and my family.*

When Rob was living with his dad
(who was an elder at The Jehovah's
Witness Hall), he decided he did not
want Rob going to church with me. He didn't want Rob to
be a part of any birthday or church celebrations. But more
and more, Rob had questions about Jesus. He enjoyed the
joy and love that he felt when he was with me and my
family. Being together and being around my family, who
loved Rob from the beginning, made his dad feel a certain
way. He told Rob to leave his house. He was confused about
salvation. I didn't know that Rob mentioned to him that he
wanted to accept Jesus Christ as his Lord and Savior.

His dad asked, "What does that mean?" Robert said, "I
will be saved!" He knew he wanted to receive salvation
from the Lord. Just then, everything that could hit the fan
did just that.

So, Rob left his dad's home and was homeless. When my
father heard about all this, he called me in his room. He told
me to call Rob and have him come to dinner. At dinner, my
dad prayed for Rob and handed him some money. He
instructed Rob to call around to look for an apartment and
ensured him that he would help him get settled. Now, it
was my decision early one that Rob, and I would just be

friends. The way I saw it, I loved Jesus and Rob did not even know *Him*. I know some of you (with your eyebrows up) are reading this, saying, "Umm, isn't that the time you witness to him and share Jesus with him?"

But, in all honesty, I was like, "It was nice meeting you, but this will never work out." My father, the Reverend Calop Brown, an old-school, southern Baptist preacher, lived a life in segregation in Alabama for the first part of his life.

He was called the "N" word more times than he could count. That same man came to me and asked me where Rob was and why he hadn't been over to the house. I started to tell Poppa why when, all of a sudden, he looked at me and said, "Girl, don't you know that God is using you as *His* lighthouse? *He* is going to use you, and He's going to use the light *He* has placed inside of you to draw Rob to *Him*. He continued to explain, just like ships that are out at sea, they need the lighthouse to direct and guide them safely to shore when it's dark. Poppa said, "It doesn't matter what Rob doesn't believe or what he was taught. The Lord has great plans for him, and if *He* be lifted up, He will draw all men unto Him. Well, that was that! Poppa had spoken, and I called and apologized to Rob.

Instead of Rob getting the apartment, he decided to move in with his mother. She was not a Jehovah's Witness nor a believer in Jesus Christ. Now the picture gets more color thrown on it. To be absolutely honest, this was not a good decision at all. When Rob started living there, he changed to fit into that environment. He stayed up all night, partying and doing drugs with friends and his mother. Partying with your mom was not normal to me. She didn't see anything wrong with it. Rob no longer wanted to go to church, and he barely came over for dinner. When I asked his mom to come over, she always had an excuse.

We got mad at each other, but even madder at everyone else who saw color and had a problem with our relationship.

I realized she was not happy about our relationship, and Rob's mom refused to drive into the City of Detroit. Then when we did go out with just the two of us, there were more stares from people. Some people looked on with unbelief on their faces. Others (especially Black men) said all kinds of horrible, mean and unnecessary things out loud about us or directly toward Rob. For me, it was fight time. But Rob would just grab my hand and we would talk, walk, dance, eat, laugh or look at each other like we were the only ones there. It was very difficult for me to hear black men comment with so much anger. It was hard for me to deal with the way his mother felt about me. It was straight racism, and it was right in our faces. As time went by, Rob did move into his own place. Praise God!

Unfortunately, his mom and I never really had a relationship. I did not like her, nor did I trust her. Because of my strong feelings toward his mom, it built and created a space between us that had never been there before. Neither one of us wanted to be there. So, we did what we always did: we talked! We shared our true feelings. We got mad at each other, but even madder at everyone else who saw color and had a problem with our relationship. Rob and I asked questions and waited for each other to answer honestly. Hate and prejudice had stepped in, and we had to deal with it head on. We both knew that our hearts and lives were connected for a reason. We were going to live it the best way we could—*together*! With or without anyone's approval, comments, suggestions, ridicule, acceptance or racist thoughts, we were staying together and fighting for each other.

So, it was time to plan our wedding! Oh, how excited I was. So was my father. Even Rob's dad (who apologized and was a part of his life again) was looking forward to being a part of the ceremony. I'd dreamed of getting married on a boat. So, my sister and I planned the wedding to be on the Nordic Princess Cruise ship. It was amazing and absolutely beautiful. Our reception was the Captain's Ball. Although I did not want his mom there, I agreed that she could come. But she couldn't stay on the boat with us and my family. The hurt and the anger were still there, even on that beautiful day. I couldn't shake her asking us, "Are you guys sure you want to get married *and* have kids?" She was concerned for us to have mixed kids and she worried about how the world would treat them.

However, she didn't recognize how she was treating me and her son.

After the wedding, I moved in with Rob, and both of us started new jobs. Life was great. There was blessing after blessing for the next few years, including our oldest son being born. During my pregnancy with Lil' Rob, we hit some bumps along the way. Again, I had to deal with Rob going to visit his mom but coming back home so high that he would have to go straight to bed. It was a struggle for me, especially when I was called to the ministry with my parents. I was ordained. My focus was on the Lord. Because of what was going on with our marriage, me being upset a lot, and me crying until he got home, then not speaking to each other for days, Robert, Jr. was born with a serious stomach issue called Colic. His stomach was so nervous, and he was in pain all the time. After a few months, Lil' Rob was eating and growing like a weed. As time and the years went by, I prayed and sought the Lord about forgiveness.

As the holidays and birthdays came, I knew I would eventually have to see his mom. Notice I have not mentioned that I called her "mom" (like Rob did with my mom). I didn't feel that in my heart, so I called her by her name. But I had to seek the Lord about my heart. So, yes, we always went to his mom's house first for dinner on Thanksgiving, Christmas and New Year's Eve, simply because of the difference in the food. Rob would say, "Let's go to my mom's first and snack a little there. Then, we can head over to your mom's to eat." We would both laugh and make jokes to everyone about the difference in food. We would get to Rob's mom's house, and it would be stuffing with the turkey; but at my mom's, it was dressing (prepared to taste completely different) with the turkey. At his mom's, there was green bean casserole; but at my mom's, it would be collard greens. His mom had mashed potatoes; there were candied yams at my mom's. For dessert, his mom had pumpkin pie; but it would be a mountain of dessert at my mom's, starting with sweet potato pie. One thing about it, Rob and I enjoyed being with family, especially now that we had our own.

In my time of seeking the Lord, I found myself in repentance more and surrendering my will unto *Him*. In the midst of searching my heart and crying out to the Lord because I did not want to carry unforgiveness anymore, I refused to allow anger to cause me to become bitter. Matthew 11:26 was one of the Scriptures I spoke daily. I want the Father to forgive me of my sins, my iniquities and my transgressions. Without sharing with Rob,

As I drew closer to the Lord, and my relationship grew in Him, my surrender was not a struggle anymore.

I fasted for days. I laid before the Lord for myself. Many times, we point the finger at someone else: our spouses, our family members or our co-workers. But the old folks used to say, "It's me, oh, Lord, standing in the need of prayer."

As I drew closer to the Lord, and my relationship grew in Him, my surrender was not a struggle anymore. Before, I went back and forth with God and tried to negotiate with Him. But I yielded my ways unto the Lord. I gave in and let go of past hurt, disappointments and words. Just as it states in Ecclesiastes, there is a time and a season for every purpose under Heaven. Those were my questions, "Why did this take so long? Why didn't I do this earlier in our relationship?" But I (we) have to go through it to get to what *He* prepared for us. Rob experienced an incredible shift in his life.

He got laid off from his job, and he collected no unemployment. There was no money coming in. We lost our car and we barely paid bills. We received eviction notices. But God had to allow all of it to get Rob's

This is why I had to really surrender all to the Lord, so that the reconstruction could take place in the heart, mind and spirit.

attention. There was no more partying all night, getting high with his mom and friends or coming home late. He didn't even have money to do any of it. Before I knew it, Rob was also in repentance, surrendering all to the Lord. One night, I overheard Rob in the room praying and talking to the

Lord. All of a sudden, he yelled aloud, "Here I am! Use me, God." I went to my knees in the hallway and praised God. I sang Thanksgiving to *Him*. It was all necessary. As Habakkuk 2:3 says, *For the vision is yet for an appointed time.* Hallelujah! God is always on time. His timing is perfect, even when it came to our second son being born.

When my father passed away, my mother decided she would ordain me as pastor over the ministry. What an honor and what a responsibility to lead, feed, guide, teach and disciple the people who my father was the shepherd over for so many years. Rob was so excited and incredibly supportive. This is why I had to really surrender all to the Lord, so that the reconstruction could take place in the heart, mind and spirit. At the end of it all, my mother in-law had to see Christ in me. When she and I started back talking, I saw so much hurt in her. It was a lot of rejection and abandonment. The Lord showed me so much so that I would intercede and come against bloodline curses, addiction, hatred, racism, fear, manipulation and control.

With Rob and I being an interracial couple, we both had to come against and bind on both sides of our family. When you look at our bloodline, some of his ancestors owned some of my ancestors as slaves. We understood that all of it had to be broken in the name of Jesus. Our boys would not be attached to any of it! Rob is right by my side, as I am

This is where I am amazed how the Lord set all of this up. leading the people and teaching, preaching, helping, feeding, clothing, traveling and being the servant *He* called me to be. Rob has his own place in God. He is confident that he is married and in love with a Black woman, a female pastor that shepherds a multicultural congregation. This is where I am amazed how the Lord set all of this up.

From the two ships coming together, to not being sure we should stay together because he didn't have a relationship with Jesus, to wanting to throw his mother overboard at our wedding, to standing my ground and not choosing pumpkin pie over sweet potato. I fell on my face in complete surrender to the Lord to change my heart so I would be an example for others.

Today, we have two incredible boys, Robert, Jr. and Joshua Caleb and we finally released a promotion and elevation from the Lord to Pastor. He would use Rob and I as *His* billboard. It is my prayer that people, the body of Christ and the world can look at us and see true love and God's glory. A billboard is used for marketing and advertising. It gives direction. That is exactly how the Lord is using us. I am extremely grateful to the Lord for all that *He* has done. He is faithful! What the enemy meant for evil, God completely turned it around for our good. If I could make a statement that would move and shift thinking, as well as the hearts of men, it would be drugs don't see color. We do. Alcoholism does not see color. We do. Depression does not see color. We do. anxiety, fear or suicide doesn't see color. We do. It is time to check our hearts and our vision.

This is our story—in black and white.

 *Reflection Questions*

1. *Is everyone in your picture, painting or circle the same color or race? If so, why?*

   _____

   _____

   _____

2. *How can you posture your heart for change?*

   _____

   _____

   _____

3. *What have you surrendered unto the Lord?*

   _____

   _____

   _____

4. *Who are you a lighthouse or billboard for?*

_____

_____

_____

5. *How has racism slid into your thoughts, words or actions in your life?*

_____

_____

_____

ABOUT THE AUTHOR

Pastor Lisa Reeves

While many are called, few are chosen. Affectionately known as "Pastor Lisa," Lisa R. Reeves is crystal clear on her mission and her mandate: to save the lost, help them find freedom through Jesus Christ, and operate in their divine, God-given purpose. A product of two pastors, Pastor Lisa found new life in Christ only after she went blind in the midst of her riotous living. Committed to turning her life around for the greater good, little did she know that she had already experienced a divine intervention and spiritual awakening.

Accepting her call to pastor in August of 2009, she has served diligently as pastor of Hope Outreach Ministries until the Lord instructed her to change the name to New Wine Restoration Ministries, a multi-faceted ministry that demonstrates love in action, in April 2022. Reaching out to those in desperate physical and spiritual need, Lisa spends time feeding the homeless in the downtown Detroit and surrounding areas and pouring her heart out to women who are imprisoned—spiritually, emotionally and physically. A prophetic voice and mentor to women of all ages and backgrounds, she has been fortunate to walk through numerous doors of opportunity—including traveling with ministerial leaders around the nation, speaking at women's conferences and hosting her own transformational signature events. A former broadcaster on Gospel 1440 WMKM radio station, her voice and her words of wisdom still speak loud and clear in the lives of those she has impacted worldwide.

For booking or speaking engagements, email lreeves0628@aol.com or call 586.287.4565.

DEFEATING THE PLANS OF THE ENEMY

Dr. LaToya R. Thurmond

Marching to the beat of the drum others came with a need for validation, anxiety, stress and obsession with pleasing people.

Living your life for others can be a rigged fight. Whether you win or lose, rejection seems to be your prize. It can be like standing in a whirlwind of constant reminders of how much further you need to go, while battling the silent treatment, dismissal, non-acceptance, neglect and abandonment. If you are not careful, you will tolerate and accept anything just to feel loved, only to be quickly reinjured. It took a while for me to notice that this vicious cycle was hidden, lurking, waiting to throw me back into a never-ending fight.

At the tender age of six years old, I became a people pleaser, striving for acceptance and identity. I traveled to auditions in a silver Silverado in the back seat without air conditioning, the wind smacking me in the face and violently blowing my curled bangs. It seemed as if the wind's mission was to destroy everything in its path. We were on another long car ride with the hot sun beaming on my sweaty cheeks pressed against the plastic dry cleaning bag. There had to be three or four changes of clothes in that plastic bag. While trying to keep it all together on the car ride, the real pressure was ahead of me.

Quickly setting into the mode of people pleasing, I continued on the journey of sacrificing my true identity and voice...

I was overwhelmed by memorizing lines, speaking at the right speed, "slow down", "sound excited", "stand here", "sit there", "no not there...here." I can't forget about the bright lights that exposed all of my imperfections and sent me into full examination. "Let's fix your bangs. Oh, wait...your collar needs to be fixed. Oh, your buttons are a little twisted."

There was no time for fun. This was serious business, and everyone seemed to be in a rush. I needed to be camera ready and picture perfect. Quickly, I discovered that getting it right brought excitement, whereas making mistakes bought frustration.

I remember that day like it was yesterday. "Look at me, LaToya, and say, 'My mom makes the best spaghetti!'"

"But she doesn't make the spaghetti," I replied.

I didn't happen to like my mom's spaghetti, and I wasn't afraid to be honest about it. Quickly, my father redirected me, repeating my line with total exaggeration.

"Snook, say it. "My moooommmmm makes the best spaghetti!" I remember the brief pause as I thought long and hard about my mom's spaghetti.

"But she doesn't make the best spaghetti," I replied.

It wasn't that I did not understand what I was being asked to say. It was the fact that my opinion was she *didn't* make the best spaghetti. There was no way I could agree to that. But in that moment, I said what I was asked to say. I learned the art of saying what people wanted to hear out of fear. I continued to grow and develop under pressure, constant critiques, and too few affirmations. I pushed myself to the max, seeking approval and validation while overcoming obstacles, hurdles setbacks.

Quickly setting into the mode of people pleasing, I continued on the journey of sacrificing my true identity and voice in exchange for what I thought would make others happy. Unaware that God had given me the grace to build and operate in multiple arenas, I feared I would be misunderstood. Failing to realize that it was "grace" upon my life, I ran in my own strength, focused on the people, and often played it safe out of fear of rejection. The enemy had a plan to restrict my movement at a young age by way of fear of other people's opinions. This fear caused me to internalize and overthink conversations, interactions, expectations and relationships, which made it more challenging for me to walk fully in my purpose.

With the pressure to produce, and the lack of being affirmed, I questioned my abilities often. My constant questioning developed insecurities, making it difficult to excel. Stuck in mediocrity, I found myself boxed in and feeling safe in my limited space.

> *"The thief comes only to steal and kill and destroy; I have come that they may have life, and have it to the full."*
> –JOHN 10:10

How can a thief continue to rob you from your possessions?

The thief would need to keep you blinded from knowing that a robbery has even occurred. According to consumer affairs, cybercriminals are targeting more Americans who are working remotely from home. This concern requires that individuals put in place protective measures to safeguard their identity. In addition, consumer affairs recommended that you make a routine effort to search for any warning signs. Cybercriminals typically target individuals who are not aware and unlikely to report suspicious activity.

The enemy often uses deception and distraction to make you lose sight or awareness of who you are.

"You are the light of the world-like a city on a hilltop that cannot be hidden. Neither do people light a lamp and put it under a bowl. Instead, they put it on its stand, and it gives light to everyone in the house. In the same way, let your light shine before others, that they may see your good deeds and glorify your Father in heaven."
MATTHEW 5:14-16

You become an easy target when you don't realize who you are in Christ and what you possess. It's easy to overlook that something is missing when you never knew you had it. The enemy often uses deception and distraction to make you lose sight or awareness of who you are. He violently attacks your self-esteem and confidence in an effort to blind you from seeing your giftedness. The enemy doesn't fight fair. He will go as far as enlisting your loved ones unconsciously to give destructive criticism, designed to paralyze you mentally and emotionally.

Stay Alert

Have you ever heard that when a child falls, and he or she is seriously injured, it requires that you control your emotions? Your ability to keep calm is what will help the child recover from the painful experience. I must admit that I lived a big portion of my life like a child falling off of her bike, then quickly hopping back on, pushing past scratches, cuts and deep wounds. I learned to push past my emotions.

They would only slow me down. Unaware, of my injuries I kept it moving.

It is easy to go about life being unaligned and unaware of your God-given assignment when you normalize what brings you pain and suffering. Desensitized, and unable to connect with my authentic self and emotions, I learned to function in dysfunctional cycles and grew numb to my emotional scars.

Being sensitive and easily broken is identified as a negative characteristic. I was about ten years old when I learned how to suppress my emotions.

"Toy, quit all that crying. If you keep crying all the time you won't have tears when you really need them," they told me.

In order to survive, I had to armor up with what I call a Teflon vest. Unfortunately, I found that I needed this vest to protect myself more from family than I did from people in the streets. This Teflon vest blocked the comments that made me guilty and ashamed of the favor and hand of God on my life as He allowed me to succeed. It also protected me from family who loved to sow discord by playing the comparison game with intention of letting me know that I was non-existent in their world. The Teflon vest was a way to block out all attempts that were intentionally made to make me feel insignificant when I had succeeded.

The enemy had been chipping away at my confidence and identity, and now he was after my mind.

It's amazing to see the amount of energy people will pour into making you feel unwanted. The Teflon vest made me feel as though I was winning the fight when, in reality, I was losing to pride and bitterness. While I had learned to block out the shots fired and shade thrown, I was internalizing everything. It caused never-ending cycles of mental anguish. I paid special attention to tones, pitches, body language and facial expressions, trying to decipher alternative meanings. While trying to cope, I internalized every interaction and comment. Some of it was just me overthinking while, at other times, I knew I was facing psychological warfare. Wearing my Teflon vest made life so much easier when I started to feel like I was experiencing psychological warfare. The enemy had been chipping away at my confidence and identity, and now he was after my mind.

I grew tired of the reconciliations and what seemed to be constant reinjuries. For me, hiding behind my Teflon vest made it easy to function in dysfunction. Somewhere in my younger years, I adopted this idea that expressing my feelings and emotions was a weakness that would only slow me down. I saw my Teflon vest as protective gear, designed to keep me safe and hidden away. However, the internal fight was ongoing, and I suffered silently. Fighting to go undetected of my internal battles, I struggled to pull it together and keep it together. However, behind the vest was self-sabotage, internalizing and the voice of the enemy. I spent countless hours fighting my way through opportunities and what I now know as my God-given assignment out of fear of rejection, criticism and not feeling as though I was good enough. After while I got so used to the fight that I didn't recognize it as a struggle. It was just something that I needed to do to keep myself from drowning. The enemy's plan is to exhaust you while keeping you unaware of your internal struggles.

It may be hard to accept and acknowledge all of the issues of life that are designed to violently attack and shake us from walking in destiny.

Be Aware

"Do not conform to the pattern of this world, but be transformed by the renewing of your mind. Then you will be able to test and approve what God's will is—his good, pleasing and perfect will."
–ROMANS 12:2

According to Dr. Judy Mangion, assistant professor of medicine at Harvard Medical School, heart infections can go undetected. "Because the consequences can be quite serious, it's important to know the risks and recognize the symptoms," she says.

The entire world has quickly adapted to protective measures and plans that safeguard our well-being. It is necessary to remain cautious and take extra steps to remain virus-free. COVID-19 showed up two years ago, but how long have we continued to go about life, infected by viruses that silently work to destroy our hearts, minds and destiny?

It may be hard to accept and acknowledge all of the issues of life that are designed to violently attack and shake us from walking in destiny. It takes an immense level of bravery to recognize and admit that there may be a viral infection deep within. In addition, one must release the pride to admit that we truly need God to heal and deliver us from all our sufferings that have gone unseen and unchecked.

As a little girl, I remember the saints standing up and testifying. "If it had not been for the Lord on my side, I would have lost my mind." I came to know the impact of the song *Amazing Grace* as I saw God's hand in all of my struggles.

"But you are a chosen people, a royal priesthood, a holy nation, God's special possession, that you may declare the praises of him who called you out of darkness into his wonderful light."
–1 PETER 2:9

Identifying the Plans of The Enemy

"Be alert and sober minded. Your enemy the devil prowls around like a roaring lion looking for someone to devour."
–1 PETER 5:8-9

I dreamt about it more than I had liked. This time in the dream, I was pregnant and waddling in the hospital halls. The intensive care unit seemed to be abandoned, yet full of incoherent people who had just been casted for the walking dead. As I wobbled to each person, trying to gain insight as to what was happening, I received nothing but silence. Suddenly, the shadow appeared, and the windows were covered from top to bottom. As I took a closer look, I saw the scales of a black anaconda. As it continued to circle around, its gigantic head activated the automatic hospital door as it peered into the building.

The enemy comes to paralyze you with fear so he can restrict your movement and silence your voice in order to prevent you from walking in purpose. My identity, and who I believed myself to be, was built up in the opinions of others. I had to go from seeking the approval of others to seeking God's approval. The enemy had a plan to abort my purpose by silencing my voice and stealing my true identity.

Defeating the Enemy's Plan

I shall not die, but I will live and proclaim what the Lord has done.
–PSALM 118:17

It was the morning of April 24, 2007. I felt like I had lost all control of my body from the neck down. This was my second time having a C-section and something didn't feel right. I went into a panic as I felt like the wind had just been knocked out of me. As I lay on the operating table under the beaming light, gasping for air, a death sentence is what they gave me. There are those who sound as if they are in panic and others who sound as if this is just another day in labor and delivery.

Unable to move or respond, I remained conscious and aware of every remark, comment and sound in the operating room.

"Keep it moving."

"Her oxygen levels are getting lower."

"Come on! Breathe! You're going to make it."

"She is going to die and there is nothing we can do."

"We have to take her to the cardiac unit. She is only breathing at 17%. We need to get her to the cardiac unit."

Another member of the labor and delivery team hurled out, "Our job is to deliver the baby and she will not make it to the cardiac unit."

Unable to move or respond, I remained conscious and aware of every remark, comment and sound in the operating room. Again, my voice had been stripped. I still had no clue what was happening. In and out of consciousness, I still couldn't quite grasp what had gone wrong. I felt as though the wind had been knocked out of me and I could not catch my breath. I knew from the sounds of my surroundings that things still were not looking good. Exhausted from the long fight to breathe, my faith wavered.

Suddenly, I heard the curdling crying of a baby. Still struggling to breathe, the nurse made one final suggestion that made it more evident of my expected end.

"She's not going to make it. Bring the baby over so she can see her."

Feelings of suffocation pushed my anxiety into high gear, sending me into extreme panic. My inability to relax caused me to overwork myself and the oxygen that I did have. With tears streaming down my face, I came to grips with the fact that I was in a life-or-death situation. In that moment, I could choose to believe the doctors' report and choose death, or I could believe the report of the Lord. It was then in that moment that I knew I had to fight.

I was in a physical fight for my life and, yet again, my mind was in a war zone.

The thief cometh not, but for to steal, and to kill, and to destroy: I am come that they might have life, and that they might have it more abundantly.
–JOHN 10:10

The medical team had no idea that they had played right into the hands of the enemy as they declared death upon my life. *But God!*

For I know the plans I have for you," declares the Lord, "plans to prosper you and not to harm you, plans to give you hope and a future."
—JEREMIAH 29:11

I was in a physical fight for my life and, yet again, my mind was in a war zone. I was experiencing battle fatigue as I struggled physically, mentally and emotionally. I wrestled with unimaginable thoughts and fears. Again, this was yet another expectation. This time, the expectation was death due to childbirth complications.

When you have been formed, fashioned and chosen for a purpose, the enemy will do whatever he can to destroy you. This medical emergency stripped me of all control and all I could do was trust God, trust in His Word, and trust that He had plans for my future. Although death had gripped me tight, I decided on that operating room table to walk by faith, not by sight.

There was a "familiar voice" who seemed to be in the fight with me. Like the raven who fed prophet Elijah, he stuck by me and encouraged me to breathe between yelling explicit language and in his moments of panic. Where everyone saw no hope, he was invested in helping me.

"I cannot just let her die."

The light beams shone in my eyes. Then, I could hear the "familiar voice" hovering over me. "I need you to help me help you."

The tears flowed at a steady stream. Unable to talk, I thought to myself, *God, please save me!*

These next set of divine instructions is what would turn this entire situation around.

"I know you can hear me. I am going to put this down your throat and I need you to fight with everything you have to breathe as I count to three. Breathe in..."

Suddenly, as he began to count, I began to replace "Breathe" with "Jesus!"

It was excruciating, but I had a few lessons in doing exactly what I had been told to do.

"Again. One, two, three. Breathe in!" I did not know how long this would last and if I would be able to make it.

"Again. One, two, three. Breathe!" I was exhausted.

For she thought to herself, "If I can just touch his robe, I will be healed."
–MARK 5:28

Suddenly, as he began to count, I began to replace "Breathe" with "Jesus!"

At the count of, "One...," I pressed my way past anxiety.

At the count of, "Two...," I pressed my way past fear.

At the count of, "Three...," I pressed my way past (yet again) the opinion and expectations of others to call on the name of Jesus.

"For I can do everything through Christ, who gives me strength."
–PHILIPPIANS 4:13

Somewhere within the moments of taking deep breaths, I drifted off to sleep.

"Then the LORD God formed a man from the dust of the ground and breathed into his nostrils the breath of life, and the man became a living being."
–GENESIS 2:7

As I gained awareness, I could hear the medical team giving vitals. "She is now breathing at seventy percent. This is another one saved."

Recovery

"You will seek me and find me when you seek me with all your heart."
–JEREMIAH 29:13

I was beginning to feel like normal, but I was still curious as to what I had just experienced. This experience was so traumatic that I was still on high alert for voices, tones and sounds. The nurse entered my room, and, in total amazement, she said, "LaToya, you had quite the scare and are so lucky to be alive."

Shortly after, I had a visitor arrive. I quickly took notice of the "familiar voice" who had introduced himself as the anesthesiologist.

"I want to thank you for helping me help you. What you experienced is something that I have never witnessed in my medical career."

When you were given the epidural, it should have numbed you from the waist down. But the medicine reversed and shut your entire upper respiratory system down, which paralyzed your lungs and caused a life-threatening situation.

When you are undergoing surgery, there is a specialized medical team. Each member performs specific functions that have a direct impact on the patient's health. The anesthesiologist had been there from the point of administering the epidural, to the point of me going numb, to the point of matters turning worst. He showed up again to help me process all that had gone wrong and to rejoice with me in surviving.

In the same way, Jesus had been there all along. He journeyed with me every step of the way. He knew every wound that I was unaware of. He knew when I had gone numb. He knew when I had lost consciousness of my true self. He knew when I walked in fear. He knew that I would have a life-threatening experience.

Honestly, I was struggling with the woman in the mirror.

He had been there all the time. Jesus saved my life!

"He brought me up also out of a horrible pit, out of the miry clay, and set my feet upon a rock, and established my goings."
–PSALM 40:2

My journey to recovery included disconnecting from places, spaces and people who would potentially interfere with my transformation. I had taken a bit of a pause, which created increased time for further introspection. Honestly, I was struggling with the woman in the mirror. I was ashamed of how I allowed my condition to go on undetected. It felt like I had literally woken up one day and noticed that I was bleeding from several injuries and was moving about life, unaware of my pain.

The Lord sent help and I was able to be vulnerable, real and a mess without being judged and held to a certain expectation. My specialized care team interceded on my behalf and spoke into my life. They reminded me that, even in all of what I experienced, and was still experiencing, there was *still yet* a call on my life. My mindset needed some major adjusting, and they were willing to get in the ring and stay in the fight with me.

The Teflon vest that weighed me down was exchanged for putting on the full armor of God. I have learned to realize my internal struggles and I have learned how it was designed to interfere with my destiny. Because I perceive that God has created and fashioned me with purpose and has *graced* me to do and be, I no longer have to walk in fear. I exchanged pleasing people for pleasing God. In my ability to perceive my destiny, I now have no regrets or shame in pursuing all of the many things God has graced me to be and do. I have also made a conscious decision to "live" and walk boldly in all He has created me to be.

Reflection Questions

1. *What cycles in your life need to be broken?*

   _____

   _____

   _____

2. *What is stopping you from pursuing your purpose?*

   _____

   _____

   _____

3. *Who is on your specialized spiritual support team?*

   _____

   _____

   _____

ABOUT THE AUTHOR

Dr. LaToya R. Thurmond

*D*r. LaToya Thurmond is a faith-based speaker, award winning author, coach, and lead pastor of Catapult Church and Family Life Center. She credits her twelve years of serving in ministry and seventeen years as a successful business owner to the anointing that God has placed upon her life. She continues to acknowledge the Holy Spirit's position as the true CEO in what she identifies as a *businesstry* (business/ministry). In addition to marketplace ministry, she is committed to using her spiritual gifts to transform the lives of children, youth and families in her community. Dr. LaToya is a visionary who helps others come to the realization that transformation is possible. She has a great passion for God's people and believes in empowering and motivating individuals to find their purpose through exploring the Word of God.

Dr. LaToya finds great joy in teaching God's people how to stand up and be strong while fighting in God's army. She is inspired by Philippians 4:13: *"I can do all things through Christ who strengthens me."* With that same Scripture, she inspires others by leading them to acknowledge that their goals and dreams can be spoken into existence and accomplished through Christ. Her goal is to help others be transformed by the Holy Spirit through a total reformation of how they think. As believers, it is important to discern God's will as you live your best life, satisfying and perfect in His eyes.

Her motto is: Follow the blueprint that God has uniquely designed for you!

As the author of *"Help: My Business Is Holding Me"* she strives to help others in developing coping strategies that will allow them to move beyond failure to a place of abundance. Through a process of realization, refocusing and relaunch, she can move you from a position of surviving to thriving.

Dr. LaToya has an incredible ability to see the future. She thinks outside the box and perceives what could be and what might be, and how it will impact the future. Her ability to create energized empowerment messages makes lasting connections and actionable takeaways. Combining her experience as a small business owner, coach, and Ph.D. in Organizational Psychology, she creates and delivers strategies and practical tips that will leave your audience inspired and ready to move forward. Dr. LaToya resides in Racine, Wisconsin with her husband, Shaun, and two daughters, Arion and Shia, along with their Boston Terrier, "Prince."

WALKING AWAY WITH MY MIND

La'Tia N. Davis

"I walked away with my mind," seems to be the phrase that I speak to myself often. Who and what you see today took a lot of pain, pressure, pursuit, pushing, pulling and fighting through seasons that were messy, yet, transformational. My grandfather was a pastor, which was my introduction to Jesus. Living the first-family lifestyle was not fabulous at all. It came with trauma, deception and *a lot* of grace; however, it made me who I am today. I never thought I would be in this position at this point in my life.

The trauma I endured as a child was enough to have me locked in a mental institution, hugging myself and singing to the sky. But God kept my mind. I had to have alcohol to wake up, to function throughout the day and to fall asleep at night. I was kept from death as I took a "trip" after smoking a blunt that was laced with angel dust. Life was brutal, and I was looking for love in all the wrong places, people and things. I lived recklessly and tried to live holy at the same time. It was a disaster due to the trauma I experienced at the age of two. As a result of that, I have done some of the stupidest things in my life. For the life of me, I cannot understand why God still chooses me. I have been through abuse, molestation and even rape—just for God to bring me out unscathed on the other side.

My favorite scripture to date is Psalm 23:4, *"Yea, though I walk through the valley of the shadow of death, I will fear no evil: for thou art with me; thy rod and thy staff they comfort me."* This Scripture helps me understand that it is just the "shadow of death"; it is not death itself. I have come through a few hard things, but it is only by the grace of God that I have been able to persevere and come through it all.

In 1997, as life continued to spiral out of control, I found myself pregnant at nineteen. I didn't find out until three months gestation. When I found out, I was alone and scared. At that moment, I had feelings of shame, uncertainty and guilt. I thought to myself, *Being a single parent will be tough!* However, I knew I had to make the best decision for my child and me. I knew that I loved the Lord and the streets. But now, my baby was priority.

Caron was born at the time he was needed the most. He saved my natural life! The night he was born, I sat cross-legged in the bed and laid him on my legs, looked him straight in his big, brown eyes, and made a vow that I would always take care of him and have his back as best as I could. I held him up to the sky (like Rafiki did Simba in *The Lion King*) and told the Lord, "You gave him to me and now I give him back to you. Please cover him and shield him from what you are not connected to. Amen."

I know it was only because of prayer and the grace that was on my life.

Caron was the cutest little twenty-one-inch-long-legged, chocolate drop with the longest eyelashes I had ever seen on a boy. He was born with jaundice and had to stay in the hospital a few days after his birth, which was really the only time he had ever been sick, outside of severe allergies and the common cold. Leaving him was the worst thing I ever had to do, so it seemed.

At the time, I lived with my mom and stepdad. After getting settled in after a few months of having him, I quickly realized that I did not want to raise him in the streets of Detroit. Having been raised by my grandparents, I moved back home with them to begin my new life as a single parent. I handled being a parent as well as I could. It was a breeze compared to what I had seen other women go through. I know it was only because of prayer and the grace that was on my life.

Today, I have two boys. Damarr is the most kindhearted person I know. Someone once told me that he is, "your heart in human form." I cannot lie. He personifies the love that Christ has for his children. That sweet peace and love, the kind of heart that hugs you with his voice and loves on you with his eyes, saying, "It's okay. I'm right here with you." He has been the calm to this season of life. I have never had to go to the jailhouse, nor did I have to be concerned about "street life activity." My main concern was who or to what they are listening.

When you become a parent, it does not come with a handbook. We do the best we can with what we have.

The only life that my boys have seen me live is that of a saved lifestyle. It's not a perfect one or one absent of tumultuous situations. But my life is one that is on purpose, for purpose. It has not been easy; in fact, it was downright brutal at times. However, during those times, it was how I lived on both sides of the front door that carried us through. They never saw men in and out of the home. Whether times were good or bad, they saw and heard me praying, worshipping and reading my Bible. I made a vow to God to live for Him when I was younger. I read the Bible and asked questions. But coming from a Baptist background, there were *a lot* of unanswered questions.

When you become a parent, it does not come with a handbook. We do the best we can with what we have. At the end of the day, what we have is all we need. I never thought I would end up being a parent. The ways my children got here were the exact ways that God intended it to be. Even though I had them at various times in my life, they still saved me. As a child, I had trouble with my reproductive system. Doctors told me I would never have children due to having endometriosis. Later, I developed ovarian cancer cells by the age of thirty, which resulted in a total hysterectomy. So, not only am I a miracle, but so are both of my children. They are truly a gift to my life.

We have been through homelessness, as well as not having enough money for food or to pay bills, but God has always come through. There were times when I had to leave my children with my mother just so I could seek the Lord for our lives. I longed for a true relationship with Him, not just a surface relationship. I wanted that deep relationship—not because of what He could do—but because of who He was. He promised to, *"never leave thee nor forsake thee"* (Hebrews 13:5b, KJV). All I know is, at the end of the day, God saves the day. What my family and I have come through was a fascinating miracle. I have always held onto the one prophecy my grandfather left me, *"You* will be the one to make it *out!"* At the time he said it, I had no idea what he meant. But now, I understand.

I never really saw myself as having much because I grew up in poverty. Even though it did not look like it, the mentality of being impoverished stayed with me. It was not easy coming up that way. I just knew that I wanted to get out of the present situation I was in. It wasn't so much about the space; it was the mentality and the emotionalism of everything I was going through. I sat in the mirror, looking at myself and saying, "I'm going to make it out of here!" Being in the mental prison I was in, I developed body dysmorphia from being called "too pretty." Being beautiful caused a lot of situations. Too many people told me, "It costs to be pretty!"

So, I covered it up with makeup because I did not feel like I was beautiful inside, although people told me every day, "You're so amazing! You're so pretty! You're always dressed in these pretty, frilly dresses and you're just so beautiful!" I did not like being beautiful. I thought that if I made myself look like a clown with big hair, it would turn people away from me. But it didn't. It drew them closer. It was during this time that Holy Spirit spoke through someone I did not know and told me I was living a fraudulent life. From there, #NoFradulentLiving was birthed. I began living in the truth of who God created me to be, *the natural me.* No wigs, make-up only on special occasions, and dresses pertaining to my comfort level. I am free from the perception of others and how they feel about me!

The instances that you have just read about shaped me into the woman I am today, which paved the way for me to push through what I feel to be the biggest fight to date. During the 2020 pandemic, I watched "Quarantined with

Lavell" every Thursday. I did not watch a lot of TV; this was an Internet-based show. I liked the content of the show due

Her faith and belief in God, and His Word, was going to heal her son, despite what the doctors said.

to the humor, the interviews and Bible studies. One Thursday, he interviewed a young man named Vincent Rutley. He talked about how he became a quadriplegic due to a car accident. I listened to that interview with great intent. I listened to how God spared his life. The most intriguing part of the interview was the part where his mom declared to the doctor, his body and in his hospital room, "We thank you for the message, but we don't receive that." She believed that her son, *"shall not die, but live, to declare the works of the Lord"* (Psalm 118:17, KJV).

She would not back down from what she believed in. Her faith and belief in God, and His Word, was going to heal her son, despite what the doctors said. She told the doctors she believed God more than she believed what the doctors were telling her. She knew that her son would live. That portion of the interview rang out to me. As he told his story, I wept because I thought about how the faith of a mother could be that strong during the most vulnerable time in her life. At that moment, I could not fathom going through anything that massive and being that strong. She did not break. She stood on the word that he would not die, but he would live. I was so blown away and enamored by his testimony. He was acting and living his best life, he is married, and still creating movies and plays. I thought about that interview all that night. I know it was her prayer life that got her through. It was the fact that she was a mother, and she was not going to plan her son's funeral. Her strength in the Lord got her through. She walked out Hebrews 11:1: *Now faith is the substance of things hoped for, the evidence of things not seen.* Mrs. Rutley became a major influence in my life. Little did I know that, a few days later, I would be standing in her shoes, using her words as the source of my strength.

October 26, 2020, was a normal day. My son Caron (who was twenty-three at the time) had just got home from working the midnight shift. He showered, made breakfast, and laid down for the day. Damarr got up for school, and I went to the basement to work on a client's garment. This day did not seem odd at all. It was normal. The boys got pizza later in the day, and I was still working. I had been preparing to move, so the walls were bare. I threw away the furniture and stacks of boxes were up against the wall. Later that evening, I was on a call with my Sister Circle, praying past the midnight hour. Once the prayer ended, we lingered on the call for a bit, singing hymns. Not less than twenty minutes later, I received a call from who I thought was Caron.

Instead, it was a work colleague, saying that Caron was sick and that I needed to come quickly. I called my sister back, who I had been on the phone with, and told her to pray. As I got dressed, my body felt as if it were surging with electricity. I was in shock. I do not remember walking out the door or driving. But I remember showing up and seeing the EMT doing chest compressions, yelling at me and asking about drugs and medications he may have taken. This was the most traumatizing thing to see. Yet, it had not hit me that my son's life was in danger.

As they closed the door to the ambulance, I just stood there. Eventually, his boss asked if I needed someone to drive me. I declined. His coworker told me that Caron complained of a headache, passed out and began to aspirate, only to regain consciousness for a moment to unlock his phone to have his colleague call me. Then, he lost consciousness again.

He coded three times. During the ambulance ride, they were able to regain a pulse.

That was a miracle in and of itself. He coded three times. During the ambulance ride, they were able to regain a pulse. As they wheeled him in, it still had not hit me how serious this situation was. I waited in the waiting room for what seemed like days. I was stoic and had already prayed and asked God to cover and heal him. I still did not know what was going on and how severe he was. Once they got him stable, Dr. Rice called me back to the "room." You know, the room where you receive the sad news. It still had not struck me.

She spoke in the softest, yet sweetest, sad voice you could imagine. Dr. Rice started the conversation off with, "I am sorry to have to meet this way. Is there something I can get you?"

My son shall live and not die to declare the works of the Lord, and I am not planning his funeral.

I said, "No. How is Caron?"

"With the type of bleed that your son has on his brain, we don't expect him to make it through the next twenty-four hours." The moment she said the word, "bleed..." I felt the same shock flow through my body that I felt when I got the initial call. It was at that moment that I knew this was serious. Her voice got low, but I could see her lips moving, like a movie scene. At that time, I heard Vincent's voice, speaking the words that Mrs. Rutley had spoken to the doctor on his behalf. I said what I heard in my ear.

I said, "With all due respect, Dr. Rice, I do not receive that report. I choose to believe the report of the Lord. My son shall live and not die to declare the works of the Lord, and I am not planning his funeral."

She tried to convince me that my son was going to die and that there was nothing more that she or her team could do. Caron had a faint pulse and he needed to be sent to University of Michigan for further care. I listened to everything she had to say and even told her that I respected her position and degrees. But the Lord was going to manage this from here. She looked at me as if I were insane. By the time our conversation was over, the response team, security, police and what was the entire ER team were waiting for us at his room. As I walked in to see him, I looked at him. I immediately knew he was fighting for his life. He was cold and gray, and he had tubes everywhere. I bent down and whispered in his ear, "You only have one choice, and that is to live, son. You shall live and not die to declare the works of the Lord." I still had not reacted to what was happening, and I did not want to. He needed me to be his voice and be strong for him in that moment. As they were prepping him to be transferred, my aunt, who is an RN, arrived. As she looked at him, she broke down. I allowed her to have a moment, then quickly told her, "God is going to heal him. So, we will not be crying because he shall live and not die to declare the works of the Lord."

Once we arrived at U of M Hospital, Caron was rushed right into surgery to stop the bleeding. I met with the neurologist shortly after and his aneurysm was downgraded to a ruptured AVM – Stroke (Arteriovenous Malformation, an abnormal tangle of blood vessels connecting arteries and veins, which disrupts normal blood flow and oxygen circulation. It happens when a group of blood vessels in your body forms incorrectly. This usually happens during development before birth or shortly after.) Both are serious, but this change in diagnosis gave him a better chance of survival and recovery. This stroke left him paralyzed completely on his left side with a drain tube in his head to regulate the fluid, a trach that was breathing for him 100%, and a feeding tube in his belly. Once he was placed into ICU, while he laid there with his life hanging in the balance, I heard the Lord clearly said, "The miracle that you were looking for regarding Carl? I am going to make Caron the miracle your family needs to see."

I had been praying for my cousin Carl to be healed, but the Lord and Carl had other arrangements. Carl passed away in December of 2019. In fact, he was the seventh family member to pass away, and I was determined that Caron would not be the next. I did not bend nor break while God was speaking. I stood under the word that was being given and sprang into action immediately with prayer, praise and worship right there in his room. I knew he would live because God made me a promise. I remained steadfast and unmovable in what He said. I waited a few days to take to social media, in fear of exposing him at his most vulnerable state. However, I needed help praying.

I began by simply asking for prayers. It turned into me updating social media by the day and posting what we were believing for from God. This was all going on during the pandemic and the hospital did not want extra people there.

Only one visitor per day was allowed. After taking to social media, prayers, cards and love poured in from all over the globe. Friends told their friends who told their friends. He went from being in a coma to trying to sign his name. I watched God perform the miracle that He promised He would right in front of my eyes in Caron's life.

Walking through this in real time was, and still is, not easy. It was as if I birthed my baby twice, first naturally, then spiritually. I had to war against the enemy in the spirit realm to bring him back from death's door. I was determined to not allow the enemy to have him or his body. Caron had to learn how to walk and talk all over again. While walking through this season, there were times I wanted

Although we watched God perform a miracle before our very eyes, we still have a way to go.

to give up. But I couldn't. Both of my boys depended on me. After all, this was Damarr's senior year of high school. We needed to focus on him maintaining his grades to finish on time. The lack of rest and concern for me and his brother took a toll on him; however, he finished and received his diploma. I am extremely proud of the man he has become.

Although we watched God perform a miracle before our very eyes, we still have a way to go. We are now in a season of recovery. It is time to recover everything that the enemy thought he stole. If it had not been for a prayer life behind closed doors, pastors, friends and determination, *I would have lost my mind*. I gave up my life in exchange for taking care of my children, and I would do it again, if necessary. Becoming a caregiver to an adult man child was not easy. Some days, I wanted to walk away and never come back. But mercy wouldn't allow it, and grace made me stay.

No one talks about life after caregiving, especially if you are directly affected and related to the person you are caring for. You must grieve what you lost during the process and what is still yet living is traumatic for the person rendering the care. Traumatic brain injuries can change a person's character, emotions and mannerisms. Their quality of life has now been compromised and life must be lived a different way, with added precautionary measures always set in place. We overcame the enemy's plan to rob Caron of his life. But God had another plan. Saving his life and restoring our family is all God's plan. We all are still healing and looking forward to what is next. Now that graduation is over and Caron is on his feet, working and taking care of himself, it is time for this mama to heal!

Reflection Questions

1. *Would you have been able to give up your life, career and social life to take care of your adult child? Why/why not?*

_____

_____

_____

2. *How would you manage being in the position of waking up in ICU?*

_____

_____

_____

3. *What is the most important life lesson you have learned regarding being obedient?*

_____

_____

_____

ABOUT THE AUTHOR

La'Tia N. Davis

La'Tia Davis is a professional actress, vocalist and speaker dedicated to initiating change through her craft. Although her theatrical and vocal training began at a young age, Davis first caught the attention of industry leaders as a background vocalist for many national artists such as Joseph Derrico & Latter Rain, LeAndria Johnson, William Murphy, James Fortune and Ernest Pugh to name a few. Davis made a buzz from her breakout leading role in the hit stage play, "Dear Future Husband."

La'Tia birthed the #NOFRAUDLENTLIVING ministry, where she encourages the message, "Why live a *lie* when you can live *free?*" This movement was birthed out of the pain that she endured and experienced as a child, and even through adulthood, where she lived life through the lenses of lies and trauma. She also started a sewing company, "MadeByTLT" and became a seamstress/dressmaker during the 2020 pandemic, where her tagline is, "Covered in Beauty, Made in Prayer." La'Tia believes that the garments that she makes should be inspired by God with *you* in mind.

La'Tia loves her family and takes joy in spending time with her two adult children, Caron and Damarr. She loves Christ with all her heart and relies on her intimate relationship with Him to lead and guide her, believing that faith, love, obedience, prayer, fasting, serving, and remaining humble are the keys to any locked door. La'Tia is dedicated to the call of God on her life and ministry as she serves at All Nations Worship Assembly in Chicago, where Brandon & Cristabel Clack are her leaders.

ABOUT

So It Is Written

We help Christian female speakers and coaches write the ONE book that will expand their reach and get them to SIX figures in record time! Period!

As the leading content curators for six-figure authorpreneurs and entrepreneurs, So It Is Written is best known for helping them package and leverage their expertise into a bestselling book, which amplifies their brand, accelerates their paydays and attracts bigger opportunities!

Let us help you brand in excellence as an author and entrepreneur so you can develop multiple streams of income from just ONE book!

Call us at 313-777-8607 today or email info@soitiswritten.net for more details about our services. We look forward to working with you to make your project one of excellence!

www.ingramcontent.com/pod-product-compliance
Lightning Source LLC
Chambersburg PA
CBHW060322130626
46553CB00003B/887